THANK YOU FOR SHOPPING!

BY ERIKA KUHN AND JUSTIN BORAK

FOR PRODUCTION INQUIRIES
UNITED STATES AND CANADA
info@concordtheatricals.com
1-866-979-0447
UNITED KINGDOM AND EUROPE
licensing@concordtheatricals.co.uk
020-7054-7298

Each title is subject to availability from Concord Theatricals Corp., depending upon country of performance. Please be aware that *THANK YOU FOR SHOPPING!* may not be licensed by Concord Theatricals Corp. in your territory. Professional and amateur producers should contact the nearest Concord Theatricals Corp. office or licensing partner to verify availability.

No one shall make any changes in this title(s) for the purpose of production. No part of this book may be reproduced, stored in a retrieval system, scanned, uploaded, or transmitted in any form, by any means, now known or yet to be invented, including mechanical, electronic, digital, photocopying, recording, videotaping, or otherwise, without the prior written permission of the publisher. No one shall share this title(s), or any part of this title(s), through any social media or file hosting websites.

For all inquiries regarding motion picture, television, online/digital and other media rights, please contact Concord Theatricals Corp.

MUSIC AND THIRD-PARTY MATERIALS USE NOTE

Licensees are solely responsible for obtaining formal written permission from copyright owners to use copyrighted music and/or other copyrighted third-party materials (e.g. artworks, logos) in the performance of this play and are strongly cautioned to do so. If no such permission is obtained by the licensee, then the licensee must use only original music and materials that the licensee owns and controls. Licensees are solely responsible and liable for clearances of all third-party copyrighted materials, including without limitation music, and shall indemnify the copyright owners of the play(s) and their licensing agent, Concord Theatricals Corp., against any costs, expenses, losses and liabilities arising from the use of such copyrighted third-party materials by licensees. For music, please contact the appropriate music licensing authority in your territory for the rights to any incidental music.

IMPORTANT BILLING AND CREDIT REQUIREMENTS

If you have obtained performance rights to this title, please refer to your licensing agreement for important billing and credit requirements.

THANK YOU FOR SHOPPING! was first presented as a developmental reading at West Virginia University (Josh Williamson, Director of the School of Theatre and Dance) in Morgantown, West Virginia, on March 24, 2024. The project's faculty advisor was Aubrey Sirtautas. The production was directed by Erika Kuhn, with music direction by Spencer Hansen and lighting design by Justin Borak. Stage directions were read by Ethan Maxwell. The stage manager was Rachel Rock. The cast was as follows:

MAEVE	Faith King
HARPER	Veda Wheeler
DREW/DYLAN	Newton Sweeney
BLAKE/DIANA/RANDY/OLLIE	Kenzie Wasson
JESSE/JOAN/KIRBY	Ripley Hoffmaster
JORDAN/ALEX/SHANE	Matthan Elijah
ANNA/LIV	Reilly Wilcox
BROOKE/RILEY	Natalya V. Wood
THE MAN BEHIND THE MILK	Ethan Maxwell
BILL/TONI/CHAD	George Wagner
CRAIG/BROCK	Chase Kipps
JULES	Justin Borak

For Kurt: loving father and perpetual supporter.
We can still hear you in the hum.

CHARACTERS

THE REGISTERS

MAEVE – A young woman whose family owns the local grocery store. Her father, the patriarch of the family, has just passed away. She's figuring out what to do with her life. Female.

HARPER – Maeve's ex-best friend from high school. After getting a big scholarship, she left town and moved across the country for a fancy business school. She comes back to town because she needs to talk to Maeve. Female.

DREW – The leader of a group of teenagers who cause havoc in the grocery store parking lot. Any gender.

BLAKE – One of the teenage troublemakers. Any gender.

JESSE – One of the teenage troublemakers. Any gender.

JORDAN – One of the teenage troublemakers. Any gender.

THE DAIRY AISLE

ANNA – A young woman who has fallen hopelessly in love with the man who stocks the milk in the dairy aisle. Female.

BROOKE – Anna's best friend, who pushes her to go after love. Female.

THE MAN BEHIND THE MILK – The man who stocks the milk at the store. Male.

THE CANNED GOODS AISLE

BILL – An old pro and longtime employee of the store. Male.

CRAIG – An excited but nervous new employee at the store. Male.

THE PASTA AISLE

DYLAN – Riley's partner, incredibly nervous about their families meeting for the first time tomorrow. Any gender.

RILEY – Dylan's partner, trying to get Dylan excited about their upcoming meeting of the families. Any gender.

THE GREETING CARD AISLE

ALEX – A young person trying to figure out how to express their love. Any gender.

JOAN – An older woman who helps Alex navigate their feelings. Female.

THE MEAT AISLE

SHANE – A bro and a recent vegan. Male.

BROCK – A bro and a lover of meat. Male.

CHAD – A bro and a lover of meat. Male.

THE BAKERY

LIV – One of Sadie's bridesmaids and Diana's best friend. Ruined the wedding cake earlier that day. Female.

DIANA – One of Sadie's bridesmaids and Liv's best friend. Is trying to save Sadie's wedding and Liv's sanity. Female.

NOTES ON THE PLAY

The play takes place in Maeve's family's grocery store. Each scene shifts to a different aisle and section of it. These shifts can be as magical or industrial as you want, but it should always feel like we are inside the store.

Cast the show with as many or as few actors as you would like. We used doubling for our world-premiere reading, but you can do this play with any configuration you want. The only actors who shouldn't be doubled are the two playing Maeve and Harper.

This play is a vignette play. For transitions, please feel free to use characters, lights, music, and scenery to mask scene changes or make them feel organic. There are scenes in "The Stockroom" that can be used as transitional devices, but please, be creative with it!

A "/" indicates where the next line of dialogue begins.
A "–" indicates that a line should be cut off before it's finished.

NOTES ON "THE STOCKROOM"

"The Stockroom" is an annex of additional scenes. While the play in its original format reads eighty to ninety minutes, the playwrights have developed these scenes to slot in OR take the place of any scene throughout the play except for "The Registers." "The Registers" acts as a constant for the play and should never be moved. If you plan to do the play for competition purposes, we recommend placing one to two scenes in between each "Registers" scene.

The play is meant to be flexible and versatile to YOUR production. Feel free to place any of "The Stockroom" scenes throughout the play or cut scenes (other than "The Registers") that you feel unable to perform with your cast. If you have any questions, please reach out to Concord Theatricals for further instruction or help.

THANK YOU FOR SHOPPING!

(**MAEVE**, *a young woman wearing an all-black suit, opens the store.*)

(*She turns the lights on, walks past the cash registers, and takes a moment at a specific one with a worn-in stool.*)

(*Just as she takes a deep breath, four* **TEENS** *rush into the building.*)

The Registers 1: Teenage Troublemakers

(**BLAKE, DREW, JESSE,** *and* **JORDAN** *enter the grocery store on a mission.*)

DREW. Mentos and Diet Coke.

MAEVE. No –

DREW. MENTOS AND DIET COKE –

MAEVE. Guys, not today.

I know my dad let you mess around in the parking lot and have fun but I really don't want to clean up.

JESSE. Yeah, Maeve, where's your dad –

(**JORDAN** *hits* **JESSE.**)

(**JORDAN** *gestures at* **MAEVE**'s *clear funeral outfit.*)

JESSE. Oh.

Yeah.

Sorry for your loss.

> (**JESSE**, **JORDAN**, *and* **BLAKE** *all chime in with "sorry for your losses" as well.*)

DREW. We loved your dad.

BLAKE. Yeah!

MAEVE. Really?

He was kinda just an old grocery store owner.

JESSE. No.

He was OUR old grocery store owner.

JORDAN. Yeah!

And he was the only person who didn't care about us making a mess in his parking lot.

BLAKE. Honestly I thought he was magic –

DREW. Blake –

BLAKE. WHAT?

Drew, think about it.

(Honestly thinking this is magic.) Every time we would throw rotten fruit at the dumpster it would just...be clean tomorrow.

DREW. Yeah, it was Mr. –

BLAKE. *(Still thinks it's magic.)* Or remember when Jordan threw their lunch at the dumpster with Jesse to see which one exploded more, a ham and cheese or a PB and J?

> (**JORDAN** *makes an explosion noise.*)

JESSE. That was awesome.

BLAKE. The parking lot is magic!

And so was your dad!

MAEVE. To some people he was.

JESSE. No!

To all people!

BLAKE. He was like Houdini –

JESSE. He wasn't literally magic –

BLAKE. Maybe though.

DREW. My mom said he was a "pillar of the community."

BLAKE. What does that even mean?

DREW. He was old and stuff.

MAEVE. Ouch.

DREW. No, like, he's always been around!

JESSE. Like the Leaning Tower of Pizzazz –

BLAKE. Or like that big green lady in New York.

MAEVE. The Statue of –

BLAKE. LIBERTY.

The Statue of Liberty.

DREW. GUYS, HE WAS RESPECTED NOT MADE OF STONE!

MAEVE. No, it's fine!

He was old and has always been around!

BLAKE. Kinda like you!

MAEVE. Guys, chill –

DREW. Blake, you can't call people old.

BLAKE. No it's true!

I heard you were a legend back in the day.

JORDAN. Yeah, my cousin –

JESSE. She lives in an apartment –

JORDAN. She said you and your friends *ruled the school.*

JESSE. Yeah, you and what's her name –?

DREW. Oh yeah, Harp –

MAEVE. *(Interrupting.)* Yeah, well, enjoy school while it lasts.

People come and go, but sometimes you get stuck.

In the purgatory that is this town.

(Awkward, long pause.)

BLAKE. Wait that sounds really scary –

DREW. So like, respectfully...

What are you doing here?

MAEVE. What?

JORDAN. Yeah, like...

Shouldn't you be with your people today?

MAEVE. *(Kinda a joke.)* I couldn't get the day off work.

Boss is a real jerk!

BLAKE. Dude he's *dead...*

JESSE. Aren't you the boss now?

Couldn't you just give yourself the day off work?

DREW. I think she was trying to be funny.

MAEVE. And it clearly worked.

BLAKE. Your dad was better at being funny.

MAYBE 'CAUSE HE WAS MAGIC.

MAEVE. I hate to break it to you...

But this is just a grocery store.

My dad's not magic.

He was just a pushover who cleaned up after you guys when you'd destroy his parking lot.

(Beat.)

(The **TEENS** *are kinda hurt by this.)*

BLAKE. *(Under their breath.)* I still think he was magic –

DREW. *(To* **MAEVE.***)* Well, that's what we do!

What we've always done!

Our friend group throws your trash at large objects.

JESSE. Yeah!

It's our thing!

DREW. *(To* **MAEVE.***)* Didn't you used to have fun with your friends?

MAEVE. Well, I –

JORDAN. Maeve, you still *like* fun right?

BLAKE. You don't like live in the store or something?

(The **TEENS** *kinda laugh.)*

*(***MAEVE** *feels defensive.)*

MAEVE. I like fun!

I have a life!

I –

I –

You know what, I don't need to explain myself to you.

You're children.

(The **KIDS** *seem to be let down.)*

(They were just trying to have fun.)

*(**MAEVE** feels bad.)*

(She tries to save it.)

MAEVE. BUT…

I do have some old apples in the back.

If you PROMISE to throw them IN the dumpster, not AT…

You can take 'em to the alley –

JESSE. SCORE.

(They start to run toward the stockroom.)

*(**MAEVE** stops them.)*

MAEVE. I'll grab them as soon as I get a chance.

I don't want you all destroying the stockroom.

*(**MAEVE** exits.)*

BLAKE. She seems sad.

DREW. She IS sad.

JESSE. But still, we get to throw stuff!

Win?

JORDAN. Huge win.

DREW. I wish there was something we could do to help.

*(**HARPER** walks in wearing business casual.)*

HARPER. Are you guys open?

JESSE. We don't work here.

JORDAN. We just kinda run this place.

DREW. Yeah, we just opened.

BLAKE. I'm the boss.

HARPER. Oh really?

That's so impressive from someone your age.

BLAKE. Excuse you.

I'm forty-seven.

HARPER. Well, you look great.

BLAKE. I use lotion.

DREW. Wait, do I know you?

Do you live here?

HARPER. Used to.

My family does, I was looking for an old friend.

Maeve?

JESSE. She's in the back –

JORDAN. – getting us rotten fruit to throw at dumpsters.

BLAKE. *(Condescendingly.)* It's a boss thing.

DREW. Are you Harper?

HARPER. Uh, yes.

How do you know that?

JESSE. Oh, you're Maeve's –

(**DREW** *covers* **JESSE***'s mouth.)*

(**DREW** *thinks quickly.)*

DREW. Do you...wanna see...Blake's office?

HARPER. Uh –

BLAKE. It's a dumpster.

HARPER. Not really –

DREW. Of course you do!

Come on!

> (**DREW** *drags* **HARPER** *out to the parking lot;*
> *the others follow.)*

The Dairy Aisle 1: The Man Behind the Milk

(**ANNA** *and* **BROOKE**, *two best friends, in the dairy aisle.*)

(*They are mid-conversation.*)

BROOKE. So he's...

ANNA. Yeah...

BROOKE. ...and you've –

ANNA. Yeah –

BROOKE. Never?

ANNA. Nope.

BROOKE. So, it's like an online thing?
Like an app?

ANNA. No, not exactly –

BROOKE. Wait, then –

ANNA. We haven't officially met. Like technically.

BROOKE. So how –

ANNA. We've interacted though!

BROOKE. Interacted?

ANNA. Yeah, like we know each other.

BROOKE. Can you just tell me already?

ANNA. You're going to think I'm stupid.

BROOKE. Okay, stupid, just tell me who the guy is!

ANNA. He's... He's the man.

BROOKE. Like...he's awesome?

ANNA. No, like, he's the man...

ANNA. The man who stocks the milk.

    (Beat.)

BROOKE. The what?!

ANNA. You know, the guy!

BROOKE. Wait, which guy though?

ANNA. The guy in the back of the cooler?

BROOKE. I mean, I guess –

ANNA. And he puts the milk in and he kind of shoves it out and down to you.

BROOKE. Yeah.

ANNA. Well, I think I'm in love with him.

BROOKE. Uh-huh.

ANNA. So yeah, that's who it is.

BROOKE. That's who you've been seeing?

ANNA. In a way…

BROOKE. In a way?

ANNA. I mean I see him but…

    I guess we don't technically see each other.

BROOKE. Because he's / the –

ANNA. / the man behind the milk.

BROOKE. Right.

    Right, so –

ANNA. So, just hands mostly, forearms sometimes, if his sleeves are rolled up.

BROOKE. But obviously –

ANNA. Obviously it's cold back there so / his sleeves aren't usually rolled up.

BROOKE. / his sleeves aren't usually rolled up.

ANNA. You get it.

BROOKE. And you haven't told anyone?

ANNA. No, because obviously it's kinda crazy.

BROOKE. Yeah.

ANNA. Yeah, like usually with love at first sight you know you sort of –

BROOKE. See the guy?

ANNA. Right?

So you see the problem.

BROOKE. Okay.

Okay.

Okay, so we just need to bring the milkman to you.

ANNA. Bring the milkman to me?

BROOKE. Yeah.

We need to see the man behind the milk, but more importantly, he needs to see you.

ANNA. I just want to be seen.

BROOKE. We *all* just want to be seen!

ANNA. Exactly.

There's just one problem.

BROOKE. What's that?

ANNA. I'm lactose intolerant.

(They exit.)

The Canned Goods Aisle 1: Don't Look Down

> (**CRAIG**, *brand new to the job, and* **BILL**, *an old pro, are both employees of the grocery store.*)
>
> (**BILL** *is training* **CRAIG** *in the canned goods aisle.*)

CRAIG. Before we get started, I just really wanted to say how much I appreciate this opportunity, sir.

BILL. Yep.

CRAIG. Like, I really, really needed this job, and I want you to know, I'm ready for anything.

BILL. Yep.

CRAIG. You know, anything you need, anything I can do to help, I'm here, I'm your guy!

BILL. Yep.

CRAIG. Do you…

> (*He laughs nervously.*)

Do you ever say anything besides "yep"?

BILL. Nope.

CRAIG. Got it.

BILL. Okay, let's get started on the basics of stocking.

CRAIG. Alright, okay!

Let's get into it!

BILL. Kid, there's no bonuses for enthusiasm.

CRAIG. You got it, boss!

BILL. Ah, jeez –

CRAIG. Sorry, I mean, okay.

Yeah.

Whatever!

Yes.

    (Beat.)

BILL. Stock comes in before open on trucks, trucks unload onto the pallets, pallets get jacked and dropped along each corresponding aisle, and sometimes endcaps –

    *(**CRAIG** is furiously writing this all down in a tiny notebook.)*

CRAIG. Jacked…and…dropped, got it!

BILL. As I was saying, stock hits the floor by five a.m. and doors open at seven.

You do the math.

CRAIG. Five plus seven equals twelve, sir!

BILL. Not like that.

    *(**CRAIG** starts scribbling something out in his notebook.)*

CRAIG. I chewed the erascr off already.

BILL. You thc nervous type, kid?

CRAIG. Not a lot.

I mean a bit!

Absolutely a bit.

But a lot?

Nervous a lot?

No way, not me.

BILL. Yep.

    *(**BILL** takes the notebook out of **CRAIG**'s hands and slides it into the pocket of his vest.)*

BILL. Now, you know FIFO?

CRAIG. Like the dog?

BILL. What?

No, like First In, First Out.

CRAIG. We get to leave first?

BILL. Jeez...in the biz it means how you rotate food.

Take this here can of beans.

We match the SKU on the shelf to the box, and we see we've got plenty of room to restock.

(Tapping a can.) Hot seller.

> (**CRAIG** *nods in awe and reaches to take the notepad out of his pocket to jot this down;* **BILL** *stops him.)*

Now lookee what we have here.

> (**BILL** *reaches into the depths of the shelf and pulls out one last dusty can of beans.)*

If this ole boy doesn't get taken out and moved to the front of the row, what's gonna happen?

CRAIG. No one can reach it –

BILL. No –

CRAIG. No.

BILL. Bad. Beans.

CRAIG. *(A realization.)* Bad beans!

BILL. Do we want bad beans?

CRAIG. Uh-uh.

BILL. So we FIFO.

> (**CRAIG** *whispers "FIFO" under his breath over and over in lieu of being able to write it down.)*

Now look at this glorious aisle.

What do you see?

CRAIG. More beans?

BILL. No.

CRAIG. ...all of the beans?

BILL. No.

CRAIG. ...beautiful beans?

> (**BILL** *snaps his hand into a finger gun.*)

BILL. Bingo.

> (**CRAIG** *pumps his fist in validation.*)

You see, each of these rows in each of these aisles are faced.

Facing is when all of the pretty little labels face out to our pretty little faces.

> (**CRAIG** *mouths "pretty little labels, pretty little faces" with his eyes closed, deep in memorization mode.*)

You got all that?

CRAIG. Yes!

BILL. Alright.

Then you're good to go.

Come find me when you're out of beans.

> (**CRAIG** *orients himself to the boxes and the shelves.*)

CRAIG. But sir, what about these boxes that have beans in 'em that are already fully stocked?

BILL. Ah.

BILL. That's when you take on upstocking.

CRAIG. Upstocking?

BILL. It's when you take excess inventory...

>(**BILL** *exits around a corner and comes back dragging an old ladder.*)

...and stock it up at the top of the shelves in storage.

>(*A look of horror spreads across* **CRAIG**'s *face.*)

CRAIG. Up?

BILL. Yep. Up.

CRAIG. Up.

Up there?

BILL. You got it.

CRAIG. Up, up, way up where it's high?

BILL. Yes. Is that a problem?

CRAIG. No!

Nope!

No no no no problem at all.

BILL. Alright then.

I'll check in soon.

>(**BILL** *exits.*)

>(**CRAIG** *looks between the boxes, the ladder, and the height of the shelf in abject terror. He is afraid of lots of things. But most so, of heights.*)

>(**CRAIG** *looks right and left, alone in the aisle. He looks for something, anything to do. FIFOs and polishes the one row of beans that* **BILL** *showed him, then runs out of things to do – besides upstocking.*)

(**CRAIG** *approaches the ladder. Touches it ever so slightly. It squeaks. He jumps. A* **CUSTOMER** *or* **EMPLOYEE** *passes by. He plays it cool and ad-libs a quick "Hello!" Or a very meek "Thank you for shopping!" He's once again left alone with the ladder.)*

(**CRAIG** *squares up with the ladder. Takes a deep breath, and before he can chicken out, jumps on the first step. Barely off the ground, he holds still, really still, and checks to make sure he's still alive.)*

(He is! Emboldened, he takes another step up. Then another. He's feeling confident, proud. He takes another step, then we watch as he looks down. He is horrified.)

(Another **PASSERBY** *crosses;* **CRAIG** *tries to call out for help but is too paralyzed with fear. All that comes out is little distressed mouth sounds and breath. The* **PERSON** *doesn't notice. They grab a can of beans, consider it, change their mind, and put it back on the shelf, label askew.* **CRAIG** *looks like he is about to have a heart attack.)*

The Registers 2

(**MAEVE** *is at the registers working, a box of apples next to her.*)

(**DREW** *rushes in from the parking lot.*)

MAEVE. You guys ran out of here quick. Still want that fruit?

DREW. What?

No, we aren't hiding anyone.

MAEVE. I didn't say –

DREW. Yes, we ran out!

We had to, uh, get our ducks in a row.

MAEVE. Right, well, have fun.

(**MAEVE** *passes the box of old apples to* **DREW** *and begins to walk away.*)

DREW. WAIT!

MAEVE. What?

DREW. I, uh,

Love old apples!

Don't you?

MAEVE. Not really?

DREW. You more of a grapes girlie?

MAEVE. Grapes girlie?

Is that a real thing?

DREW. A plum person?

A kiwi kid?

MAEVE. Drew I don't have time for produce wordplay.

DREW. It's just…

I've been coming to this store my whole life and I feel like we barely know each other!

What's your favorite fruit?

MAEVE. Uh, I guess I like bananas.

DREW. Me too!

Okay, next question.

MAEVE. I'm waiting…

DREW. What would you define as your deepest hurt?

MAEVE. Excuse me?

DREW. Too deep?

I'm, uh, thinking about majoring in psychology one day –

MAEVE. Drew, what are you getting at?

I have things to do.

DREW. Yeah, yeah, I know.

We all have things to do!

MAEVE. Yes, I'm sure you have a very busy child schedule.

DREW. I'm sorry!

I'm thinking on the fly here.

Back to fruit…

   (**DREW** *sees the box of apples.*)

One thing I love to do is pick apples, off trees, with my…friends!

WHOA!

Speaking of friends, any old friends you wished you could see today?

MAEVE. Listen Drew, I clearly don't want to talk about today.

MAEVE. It's...adult stuff.

DREW. But what if I could help?

MAEVE. That's really nice,

But I don't think my problems are your problems.

You should just focus on having fun.

DREW. But what if I –

We –

Um...

Got you something?

MAEVE. Like a gift?

DREW. No, like a surprise?

> (*We hear noise outside. It's* **HARPER**, *trying to get through* **BLAKE**, **JESSE**, *and* **JORDAN** *to come back into the store.*)

MAEVE. I'm not a huge fan of surprises.

DREW. Well then maybe...

Buckle up for this one?

MAEVE. Drew...

DREW. I was trying to be helpful I promise!

> (**BLAKE** *and* **JESSE** *enter.*)

BLAKE. We can't hold her off much longer.

How's the recon going in here?

MAEVE. Recon?

DREW. *(To* **MAEVE**.*)* Not recon.

(To **BLAKE**.*)* Not well.

I don't think this is a good idea –

BLAKE. It might be too late for that.

(**HARPER** *walks in with* **JORDAN** *behind her.*)

JORDAN. Guys, she's really fast for an old person.

HARPER. For the last time, I'm not old.

JESSE. You have your own car.

That's old.

MAEVE. Harper?

(*A beat as* **MAEVE** *and* **HARPER** *see each other for the first time in a long time.*)

HARPER. Hey Maeve.

(*An awkward moment.*)

DREW. …surprise?

HARPER. Sorry, I would've gotten here sooner but –

BLAKE. No one comes and goes without the boss's okay.

MAEVE. Well… Hi.

HARPER. Hey.

MAEVE.	**HARPER.**
You look –	You look –

(*Nervous laughter. They both try to think of something to say next.*)

MAEVE.	**HARPER.**
I love your shoes.	Your hair looks great.

(*Another beat. The* **TROUBLEMAKERS** *are not feeling it.*)

JESSE. Well this is going really well.

DREW. (*With sad jazz hands.*) Surprise.

*(**MAEVE**'s eyes dart to **DREW**.)*

DREW. So, we're gonna go.

Blake, grab the fruit.

BLAKE. Grabbing.

DREW. And you guys should...you know, catch up!

*(The **TEENS** rush out.)*

MAEVE. Drew –

DREW. BYE.

*(The **TEENS** are gone. **MAEVE** and **HARPER** are
alone for the first time.)*

HARPER. Jeez, the kids in this town are still crazy.

MAEVE. I know, right?

(An awkward beat.)

HARPER. So...how have you been?

MAEVE. Fine.

Good?

HARPER. Cool, cool, cool.

Me too.

Very...fine.

(Another awkward moment.)

*(**HARPER** looks over the candy at the registers.)*

Wow, big change in the selection.

MAEVE. I fought really hard for taffy.

HARPER. You've always loved old-person candy.

It's so messed up.

MAEVE. Taffy isn't old-person candy.

HARPER. Taffy is such old-person candy!

It's right next to the butterscotch and nougat.

You and your dad are such old souls.

> (**HARPER** *realizes what she said.*)

Sorry –

> (*An awkward beat.*)

> (**HARPER** *didn't mean to bring it up.*)

> (**MAEVE** *isn't having it.*)

MAEVE. So, what are you doing here?

HARPER. I wanted to see you.

Well, I have something to say to you.

MAEVE. Weird timing.

HARPER. I know, I heard.

I'm sorry –

MAEVE. I thought maybe I'd see you at the funeral but –

HARPER. I know I –

MAEVE. I mean what's it been, like, four years since you bailed?

Why today?

HARPER. Maeve… I didn't come here to fight.

Your dad was so important to me –

MAEVE. He was important to all of us.

HARPER. He was!

I mean, he was basically my dad too growing up –

MAEVE. He was *my* dad.

HARPER. You're right.

But he was always kind to me and it meant a lot.

I know he was yours.

And I'm so sorry for your loss.

MAEVE. Well, I've lost people before.

HARPER. I know… Your mom was amazing –

MAEVE. That's not who I'm talking about.

(**HARPER** *thinks for a moment. Realizes.*)

HARPER. Oh?

Ohhh.

MAEVE. Yeah.

HARPER. Maeve, that's not the same –

MAEVE. We made a promise, Harp.

HARPER. I know that –

MAEVE. Since we were kids.

We were gonna grow up together, get the best grades in town –

HARPER. And we did!

MAEVE. And then GET OUT.

Together.

We were supposed to go to college –

HARPER. I know.

MAEVE. Room together.

HARPER. I know.

MAEVE. Take on the world.

Mae and Harp.

Together.

HARPER. Mae, I get it.

But when your dad got sick, you decided to stay here.

You had to bail.

MAEVE. You knew I had to be close to home.

HARPER. Yeah, and when I got that scholarship I couldn't say no.

MAEVE. You could've.

HARPER. *You* could've.

I couldn't.

MAEVE. Is there a difference?

HARPER. You know there's a difference.

We couldn't afford –

MAEVE. I know that but –

HARPER. I didn't know how to tell you.

MAEVE. You waited till June –

HARPER. I know –

MAEVE. I thought we had already planned to –

HARPER. No, YOU planned to stay.

I was still figuring stuff out.

I didn't want to get stuck here.

MAEVE. Cool.

Ouch.

（**HARPER** *realizes what she said.*）

HARPER. That's not what I meant.

MAEVE. It's literally what you just said.

HARPER. You have the store.

You have a life here if you want it.

MAEVE. Well what if I still don't want it?!

HARPER. You don't?

MAEVE. I never did.

You know that – knew that.

HARPER. But you stayed –

MAEVE. I had to!

HARPER. Not everything has to fall on you –

MAEVE. *(Gesturing to the store.)* Yeah, actually, it does!

HARPER. What if it didn't have to?

> *(Beat.)*

MAEVE. What are you talking about, Harper?

HARPER. Didn't you just say you still wanted an out?

After all this time?

MAEVE. Yeah...

> **(HARPER** *pulls out a manila envelope.)*

What is that...

HARPER. It's a contract.

For ownership of the store.

> **(MAEVE** *is confused.)*

> **(MAEVE** *is pissed.)*

MAEVE. *I* own the store.

HARPER. I know but what if –

MAEVE. Get out.

HARPER. Mae, let me finish –

MAEVE. No.

You've said enough.

I'm not letting you or your fancy business friends take over my family's store.

HARPER. I'm not –

MAEVE. My DAD's store.

Get out.

(An awkward beat.)

*(**HARPER** looks hurt.)*

(She puts the envelope back in her bag and walks out.)

*(**MAEVE**, pissed off, grabs an inventory clipboard and walks into the aisles.)*

The Pasta Aisle: Impasta Syndrome

*(This scene looks at food and culture. Riley is Italian and Dylan is Lebanese. Feel free to change the ethnicity or culture of the characters to fit something that your actors identify with! Do this by changing the lines and stage directions in **bold**.)*

(We know it is called "The Pasta Aisle," but if Riley is not Italian, it is okay to set this in any aisle that fits your Riley.)

*(**DYLAN** frantically enters the **pasta section** with a cart.)*

*(**DYLAN** starts throwing box after box of **pasta** in the cart.)*

*(**RILEY**, Dylan's partner, enters the aisle, sees **DYLAN** losing it, and stops them.)*

RILEY. DYLAN!

DYLAN.

RELAX.

DYLAN. Relax?!

Riley in –

*(**DYLAN** looks at their phone.)*

Thirty-one hours and thirty-five minutes –

RILEY. Also known as tomorrow night –

DYLAN. WHATEVER.

Tomorrow night both of our families will be meeting.

RILEY –

RILEY. I KNOW.

I HEARD YOU.

I HELPED PLAN IT.

DYLAN. *(Spiraling.)* My dad is gonna talk to your dad?

LIKE WHAT?

What if our moms hate each other.

What if they bring my brother's dog and your sister is allergic –

RILEY. My sister isn't allergic to dogs –

DYLAN. BUT WHAT IF SHE IS?

WHAT.

IF.

SHE.

IS.

> (**DYLAN** *collapses into* **RILEY**'s *arms overdramatically.)*
>
> (**RILEY** *laughs.)*

RILEY. Will you chill out?

It's gonna go well!

We have all the food from your side.

DYLAN. A **Lebanese** dessert and appetizer.

RILEY. I've been working on my **falafel** making –

DYLAN. Which is –

RILEY. *(Memorized.)* **"A deep-fried ball of ground broad beans and chickpeas of Middle Eastern origin."**

DYLAN. Good.

RILEY. And for dessert we are having **Ka'ik** –

DYLAN. Which is –

RILEY. **"Which is a traditional yeasted Easter bread cookie lightly flavored with mahleb and pure Lebanese rose water."**

DYLAN. And you –

RILEY. I ordered the **rose water**.

It got in yesterday.

Dylan, we're good.

DYLAN. *(Takes a breath.)* We're good.

RILEY. This is gonna be great.

A meeting of the families.

A culture-filled dinner.

Our parents are gonna love it.

DYLAN. I told my mom you were making **Ka'ik** and she lost her mind.

RILEY. And my mom is very excited to see me make my family's famous **pasta** recipe. Which, I love you, **is not bow tie.**

(**DYLAN** *looks at the cart.)*

DYLAN. Is all of this –

RILEY. Yes, **you only grabbed bow tie.**

(They laugh and start to put it back on the shelves.)

Glad I caught it.

My dad only ever eats **ditalini** –

DYLAN. **Ditalini?**

RILEY. It's the ones that kinda look like little thick cheerios.

> (**RILEY** *finds it on the shelf.*)

Boom.

Ditalini.

> (**RILEY** *tosses the box of **pasta** to* **DYLAN**.)

DYLAN. Does it really matter if you **have the thick cheerio or the frilly bow tie–looking one?**

I mean, it's all the same –

RILEY. You can't say that tomorrow.

My parents will banish you from looking at me.

DYLAN. Like why does it matter though?

For real –

RILEY. I don't know.

It's culture –

DYLAN. It's food.

RILEY. Same thing.

DYLAN. Okay –

RILEY. Really, think about it.

All over the world, people look different, speak different, believe in different things.

Some people live in the cold, some people are constantly in one-hundred-degree weather.

People grow up in cities of eight million people and some grow up in a town where everyone knows everyone.

But what do we all do?

DYLAN. Cry?

RILEY. No.

Well, yes.

But, no.

We eat.

I always thought that was cool.

Different countries eat different things, but then different states eat different things, different towns eat different things.

I mean, every family in the world has some old dingy cookbook that they treat like it's holy text.

It's so easy to know someone through their food.

DYLAN. That's fair.

RILEY. And so tomorrow night, we aren't just having a meeting of the families, we are having a blending of cultures.

A blending of us.

We are –

DYLAN. – a smoothie.

RILEY. A smoothie?

DYLAN. Blender? Smoothie?

We're giving our family a Dylan-Riley smoothie.

RILEY. That's dumb.

I love it.

      (**RILEY** *kisses* **DYLAN.**)

It's gonna be amazing.

And our families are gonna be so excited to meet and share these dishes.

DYLAN. You're right.

You're right.

I know, I'm just nervous.

I want them to like each other.

RILEY. And they will, but first.

We need to get this perfect.

We need **basil** –

DYLAN. We have **basil** at home –

RILEY. **That's spinach.**

DYLAN. **It's green**?

RILEY. You're adorable.

Grab a few more boxes of ditalini and meet me in produce.

I'm gonna teach you how to check stems!

> (**RILEY** *kisses* **DYLAN** *on the check and walks off.*)

> (**DYLAN** *grabs a few boxes* **of pasta** *and a phone goes off in the cart.*)

> (**DYLAN** *grabs it; it's Riley's phone.*)

DYLAN. *(Calling offstage.)* Riley!

It's your dad!

> (**RILEY** *can't hear* **DYLAN**.*)

> (**DYLAN** *looks at the phone, which is still ringing.*)

> *(Takes a deep breath.)*

> *(Answers.)*

> *(So nervous.)*

DYLAN. Hello, Mr. **Bianchi**! How are y–

> *(Riley's dad talks.)*

Riley is over in produce, shopping for tomorrow night.

(Trying to impress.) **I'm over in pasta, grabbing my favorite pasta, *(Reads off box.)* ditalini!**

> *(Riley's dad talks.)*

> **(DYLAN** *seems to have won some favor.)*

I KNOW!

It totally tastes different.

Very different, it's like, who likes bow tie!

> *(Riley's dad talks.)*

I'm excited too.

I'll see you tomorrow, and I'll let Riley know you called!

Bye.

> **(DYLAN** *hangs up.)*

> *(Proud.)*

> *(They walk off with their cart.)*

The Dairy Aisle

(**ANNA** *and* **BROOKE** *are still hanging out in the dairy aisle.*)

BROOKE. Did you take it?

ANNA. Of course I took it.

BROOKE. Good.

Luckily there was a sale on Lactaid, so I'm fully stocked as well!

ANNA. Okay.

Do you really think this will work?

BROOKE. Of course it'll work!

He likes milk, you like him, ergo – this will work!

ANNA. I guess maybe I'm just a really shy person, so putting myself out there like this –

BROOKE. I think you're *definitely* a shy person.

I mean you literally fell in love with a guy you haven't met and is physically unable to perceive you.

ANNA. Oh my gosh, is that bad?

BROOKE. Oh my gosh, no, that's beautiful!

ANNA. It is?

BROOKE. Totally! Can I ask though...

ANNA. Yeah?

BROOKE. Since you're dairy-free and all, how did you first meet him –

ANNA. – haven't met.

BROOKE. Sorry, right.

ANNA. No, you're totally fine.

BROOKE. But what were you doing in the milk aisle anyway?

ANNA. I was there for you.

BROOKE. What?

ANNA. Your birthday?

BROOKE. Of course!

ANNA. Your favorite dessert is homemade pudding!

BROOKE. Oh, you made me the best homemade pudding this year.

ANNA. Well, you're my best friend!

BROOKE. And you're mine.

Now, go get 'em!

*(**BROOKE** shoves **ANNA** into the milk aisle.)*

*(Maybe we see **ANNA** put on ChapStick or fuss with her hair.)*

*(**ANNA** stalks down the aisle, peering through the shelves of milk for The Man.)*

(They spot him behind the shelves.)

*(**ANNA** stops, cracks the door open, and starts pounding a quart of milk.)*

ANNA. Mmmmm!

I love milk!

So good!

THE MAN BEHIND THE MILK. *(From behind the milk.)* That's so funny. I like milk too.

*(**ANNA** and **BROOKE** lock eyes.)*

(A victory.)

The Greeting Card Aisle: Paper Over Plastic

> (**ALEX**, *a young person, is in the greeting card aisle.*)
>
> (*They face the fourth wall with a look of apprehension on their face.*)
>
> (*They're looking for something and not finding it.*)
>
> (**JOAN**, *an older woman, arrives.*)
>
> (*She walks to the far end of the aisle and stares straight ahead.*)

ALEX. Why is this so hard?

JOAN. I was just thinking the same thing.

ALEX. Oh, sorry.

I'm just talking to myself.

JOAN. That's okay.

I do it all the time too.

ALEX. Oh.

Cool, cool.

> (**ALEX** *is trying to seem cool and not crazy.*)
>
> (*They're unsure if maybe* **JOAN** *is.*)

JOAN. What are you looking for?

ALEX. Um, I guess I don't really know.

JOAN. Maybe that's the problem.

ALEX. Ha, yeah, pretty much.

JOAN. Well, what are you trying to say?

ALEX. Uhhhh –

JOAN. You can tell me.

I'm just a crazy old person in the greeting card aisle, who better to keep your secrets?

ALEX. Um, Okay.

Okay, so there's this person –

JOAN. Ah, there's always a person.

ALEX. Yeah, so.

We're, well, we're kind of figuring out what we are.

JOAN. Isn't that curious?

ALEX. Uh, maybe?

I mean we know who we are, obviously, but I guess I just need to figure out what that is.

And I was thinking maybe like a card,

Like maybe written by a professional,

You know the professionals who put specific feelings in cards,

Maybe I could just pay like $6.95 and they'd help me say it.

JOAN. I think that's a fine idea.

You know, the greeting card aisle, they have these handy little categories...like here, "niece's birthday."

Is this person your niece?

ALEX. Ew no!

Definitely not!

JOAN. Well that's one section down...

Is this person celebrating anything soon?

(Pointing.) Birthday, anniversary, christening, graduation... Are they sick?

At my age we keep a pile of "get well soon" in the kitchen drawer.

ALEX. No, that's not it either, none of that, nothing so... specific.

JOAN. I see.

Well how about something more timeless.

Perhaps "thinking of you"?

This one here has a puppy on it, and this one has a flower.

Does your person like any of those things?

ALEX. Probably...

> **(ALEX** *opens a card and reads the generic interior.)*

"Thinking of you at this time..."

I guess, maybe I'm looking for something a little more... comprehensive?

JOAN. Here.

Blanks are only ninety-nine cents.

If you know what you mean to say, just say that!

ALEX. That's my problem.

I don't know what to say.

What are you here for?

JOAN. Oh.

Thank-you cards.

ALEX. That's nice.

That's a really simple thing to say.

ALEX. Straightforward.

JOAN. It is nice, isn't it?

It's a lovely thing to have people to thank.

ALEX. My mom always says I need to write thank-you notes.

I think it's pretty old-fashioned.

JOAN. Old-fashioned doesn't mean bad.

ALEX. No, sorry!

I didn't mean to like, call you old or anything.

(**JOAN** *smiles.*)

What are you thanking for?

JOAN. Casseroles. Plants. Visits.

ALEX. Those all rock.

JOAN. They're for all the folks who stuck with me when my spouse passed.

ALEX. Oh.

Oh my gosh, I'm so sorry.

JOAN. "I'm so sorry" is with sympathy, over by retirement cards.

(**ALEX** *thinks for a moment. Goes over to the sympathy section and starts to read some aloud to* **JOAN**.*)*

ALEX. "Sending you love and healing at this difficult time."

(**JOAN** *waggles her hand in the air with a face that says "ehhh, not the best."* **ALEX** *tries again.*)

"In this time of loss, wishing you light and encouragement…"

(**JOAN** *does a thumbs-down.*)

(**ALEX** *is enjoying the game.*)

"My deepest condolences. My heart goes out to you and yours at this difficult time."

JOAN. Not the worst I've heard!

ALEX. None of these really do it, do they?

JOAN. Not necessarily.

The written word was actually a big part of our love story.

ALEX. Was it?

JOAN. Yes.

We actually met here.

At this grocery store, not long after it opened.

ALEX. That's crazy, this place is, like, so old!

(**JOAN** *raises her eyebrows.*)

Sorry!

JOAN. *(Laughing it off.)* He was the butcher here.

And he had a laugh that could fill the store from the counter to the produce section, which used to be laid out a lot better... Back then, we had this little paper-ticketing machine.

I'd put on my best hat and get in line.

I'd hope for a long one so I could spend as much time as possible "looking things over," but mostly enjoying that laugh.

He talked to everybody so kindly.

No matter what!

ALEX. And he wrote you letters?

JOAN. Yes, in his own way!

JOAN. You see, they had this crisp white paper back there, still do, and after a while, I'd find little pictures.

Doodles on the backs of pork chops and slabs of sirloin.

They didn't stop once we got married.

They just got longer, and given to me when he came home.

Little thoughts he had throughout the day, or how he missed me.

Not in the meat anymore, of course, they kept better that way.

I keep them in the drawer now with my other cards, they bring me more comfort when I'm missing him than anything from these shelves.

ALEX. Wow.

Wow, that's really amazing.

JOAN. Maybe you don't know what to say because you're too caught up on how you're going to say it.

But take it from me, if it comes from the heart, it won't matter too much.

If you know what you feel and how you feel about this person, the simplest thing would be to just write it down.

Without any meat in it, of course.

ALEX. Thank you.

You've been so helpful.

So maybe just the blank then…

> (**JOAN** *reaches down to the bottom shelf for a box.)*

JOAN. You ever seen one of these before?

It's called a stationary set, and people my age used them all the time!

I don't have many people left to be writing to, but I'm sure you do.

Send the first letter.

ALEX. Can I send you one too?

JOAN. Me?

ALEX. Yeah, like a pen-pal thing.

You give really good advice.

JOAN. Yes. I'd like that very much.

(**ALEX** *reaches down and grabs* **JOAN** *a box too.*)

The Meat Aisle: Meating in the Middle

(The meat aisle.)

(Three **BROS.***)*

*(***CHAD** *and* **BROCK***, pumped, look through all the meats.)*

*(***SHANE** *is keeping to himself; he clearly feels weird.)*

CHAD. Ribs, Ribs, Ribs –

BROCK. RIBS.

OH YEAH.

GOT 'EM.

CHAD. BOOM.

*(***CHAD** *looks at his phone.)*

Okay, just a few more things here –

Brayden wants a steak –

BROCK. FOUND THE STEAKS.

CHAD. Brock!

SNIPER IN THE MEAT AISLE TODAY.

BROCK. *(Tossing steaks in the cart.)* I'm on fire!

CHAD. Okay, okay, what else?

Shane, you want anything?

A nice, old-fashioned piece of chicken –

BROCK. How about some beef?

You wanna burger down today?

CHAD. OH, Shane wants to burger down –

BROCK. BURGER DOWWWWWWN –

CHAD. *(Realizes **SHANE** is being quiet.)* Shane?

Burger down?

SHANE. *(Fakes it.)* Oh, yeah.

Yeah, for sure, Chad.

Burger down.

> *(**SHANE***'s "burger down" is pretty low.)*

CHAD. Brochacho, what's got you down?

BROCK. Yeah, everyone is coming to your place to watch the game.

The Snakes vs. the Anacondas!

CHAD. Gonna be the game of the century.

SHANE. Yeah, isn't it weird that they're both snakes?

> *(**BROCK** and **CHAD** look at each other and then at **SHANE**, so confused.)*

BROCK. No?

CHAD. It's freaking sick.

What's gotten into you, man?

SHANE. I DON'T KNOW.

I don't know.

Sorry man, just get me a...

You know what?

Not hungry.

> *(**CHAD** and **BROCK** are shocked.)*

BROCK. NOT HUNGRY?

CHAD. What do you not get about "IT'S THE BIG GAME"?!

SHANE. We have a ton of snacks, I'll munch on that.

CHAD. "MUNCH"?

BROCK. *(Earnestly scared.)* WHAT HAVE YOU DONE WITH MY BEST FRIEND –

SHANE. I'M VEGAN.

> (**BROCK** *and* **CHAD** *are stunned.*)

> *(A long, silent beat.)*

BROCK. You're...you're –

SHANE. Vegan.

I'm vegan.

Been vegan for like a month now and honestly...

I love it.

> (**BROCK** *and* **CHAD** *cry in pain.*)

BROCK. Now, I know you're not my best friend –

CHAD. Yeah, are you an alien?

Are you some alien wearing our friend's skin as a suit?!

> (**BROCK** *goes to* **SHANE**'s *mouth and tries to yell into it.*)

BROCK. GET OUT OF MY BUDDY –

> (**SHANE** *shoves him off.*)

SHANE. I'm not an alien and I'm no different.

I'm still Shane.

I just... I'm vegan.

> (**CHAD** *and* **BROCK** *shriek a little.*)

Oh, come on!

CHAD. I'm sorry!

BROCK. *(Earnestly.)* It hurts to hear.

CHAD. How did this –

SHANE. I was scrolling on some app and came across an ebook about it.

One of my favorite pro wrestlers recommended it and I had just finished reading that book about wolves –

BROCK. *The Strongest Wolves and How to Live like Them?*

SHANE. YEAH.

That one.

But I started reading this book and it like...made a lot of sense.

There are so many issues with meat.

The conditions the animals are in, the pain they have to go through sometimes, dude, the environmental impact livestock has!

BROCK. NO.

Meat's not plants.

Meat's not environment-al-is-ism

SHANE. Dwindling the water supply, deforestation, soil erosion!

And did you know that one cup of lentils can give you the same amount of protein as a porterhouse steak?!

BROCK. I love steak.

SHANE. I know.

Me, me too.

But, then I saw this.

(**SHANE** *shows* **BROCK** *a picture on his phone.*)

(**BROCK** *is shocked.*)

CHAD. What is it?

BROCK. It's a super cute pig.

SHANE. DID YOU KNOW PIGS ARE CUTE?

I THOUGHT THEY WERE JUST BACON.

CHAD. Okay, okay –

But what about yesterday?

We had chicken from that place –

SHANE. PeaceSeed Lotus Café.

(**CHAD** *is stunned.*)

CHAD. YOU SAID IT WAS BUFFALO WILD WINGS –

SHANE. I KNOW

I'M SORRY.

IT WAS GOOD THOUGH, RIGHT?

BROCK. I honestly really liked them –

CHAD. BROCK.

BROCK. Sorry.

CHAD. I LIKE MEAT.

SHANE. And that's totally fine!

I'm –

I'm sorry, I didn't want you to feel like I was converting you or something.

And I didn't want you to think I'm like...weird or whatever.

CHAD. You're not trying to –

SHANE. NO.

BROCK. And I don't think you're weird!

SHANE. Really?

BROCK. No!

My sisters are both vegan and they love it.

I don't usually eat the same turkey as them for Thanksgiving, but I've tried tofu 'cause of them and it's...it's okay.

SHANE. It's all good!

I don't like tofu either.

I like this.

>   (**SHANE** *grabs some PsychMeat off the shelf.*)

CHAD. What's that?

SHANE. PsychMeat!

BROCK. PsychMeat?

SHANE. Yeah, like, here's some meat –

PSYCH. PLANT-BASED.

>   (*He puts it in their cart.*)

CHAD. So you're still our buddy?

SHANE. YEAH DUDE.

You're still mine?

BROCK. For sure!

CHAD. ...yeah.

I'm happy you're doing something that makes you happy.

SHANE. Thanks bro.

CHAD. And I think...

I think in honor of a bro opening up to his bros –

WE'RE ALL VEGAN TONIGHT.

SHANE. What?

BROCK. Yeah man!

If you wanna be vegan, I support you and I'll eat some weird meat –

SHANE. DUDES.

That's awesome.

PsychMeat even does ribs!

    (**BROCK** *puts his ribs back and grabs the PsychMeat ones.*)

    (*He's shocked at how normal they look.*)

BROCK. THEY LOOK KINDA NORMAL!

SHANE. YEAH.

    (**CHAD** *puts back the steaks.*)

What about Brayden?

CHAD. Brayden can deal.

LET'S GET SOME PLANT-BASED, CRUELTY-FREE MEAT AND SNACKS!

    (*The* **GUYS** *cheer.*)

    (**BROCK** *walks out.*)

    (**SHANE** *puts his hand on* **CHAD**'s *shoulder.*)

SHANE. Thanks, man.

CHAD. I got your back, bro.

BROCK. (*Offstage.*) I FOUND THE VEGAN AISLE.

IT SMELLS FUNNY!

SHANE. That's the one!

    (**CHAD** *and* **SHANE** *run off.*)

The Registers 3

(**MAEVE** *is back at the registers.*)

(*Maybe cashing someone out.*)

(*Maybe doing the books.*)

(*Maybe just thinking.*)

(**HARPER** *walks back into the store with two milkshakes from the local diner.*)

MAEVE. I thought I told you to get out.

HARPER. And I thought you'd never say no to a best friend twist?

MAEVE. (*Begrudgingly laughing.*) You didn't –

HARPER. Of course I didn't – yet. It takes two to twist.

MAEVE. I've grown up.

I can commit to one shake flavor at a time now.

HARPER. But I got us vanilla and chocolate.

Who wants just vanilla *or* chocolate?

MAEVE. You can't just make things better with milkshakes.

HARPER. It's not just milkshakes,

It's milkshakes from the diner.

(**HARPER** *sits on one of the registers and starts to make the "best friend twist" anyway. It consists of chugging a bit of each flavor then layering what's left back and forth on top.* **HARPER** *chugs her bit, looks at* **MAEVE***, and holds out the other full milkshake.*)

MAEVE. I can't be bought.

HARPER. Just shut up and drink.

Don't make me have this brain freeze alone.

> (**MAEVE** *and* **HARPER** *have a moment.*)

> (**MAEVE** *takes the cup and chugs her bit.*)

> (*While they talk, they mix milkshakes for a little while.*)

It's still really good after all these years.

MAEVE. We were culinary geniuses.

> (*Beat.*)

> (*They slurp in silence.*)

This doesn't mean we're good.

HARPER. Maeve –

MAEVE. It's messed up.

You show up out of nowhere on the day of my dad's funeral.

For what? The scraps?

So your corporate megamart bosses can make a buck?

HARPER. It's an investment company that acquires –

MAEVE. Whatever.

HARPER. But that's not what I'm here for –

MAEVE. You never cared about this place anyway.

Or me.

Or my dad for that matter.

HARPER. I did.

Of course I did.

And for what it's worth, the funeral was beautiful.

MAEVE. What are you talking about?

You weren't even there!

HARPER. You really think I wouldn't come to your dad's funeral?

MAEVE. But I didn't –

HARPER. I was in the parking lot.

I couldn't come in.

And I didn't want to freak you out.

MAEVE. Freak me out?

HARPER. We haven't seen each other in four years, Mae.

You really wanted the first time to be there?

(Beat.)

MAEVE. Oh.

HARPER. I just didn't know the right thing to do.

I get that you might not believe it,

But he really did mean a lot to me.

MAEVE. He was a good dad, wasn't he?

HARPER. Do you remember when we had that soccer tournament across the state junior year?

MAEVE. Oh my god, yes.

My dad drove us –

HARPER. And made us stop at every roadside attraction we passed by?

MAEVE. I had no idea the biggest ball of yarn was so close!

HARPER. Right?

I still think about that huge rocking chair just sitting off the highway.

MAEVE. He always took time to notice the little things like that.

HARPER. That's why he liked the diner so much.

MAEVE. What do you mean?

HARPER. Do you remember my birthday tradition?

MAEVE. Yeah, Dad took us to the diner like he always did.

HARPER. Do you know why we always did that?

MAEVE. For the best friend twist?

HARPER. No. Well, yes but –

Your dad kept my birthday marked on the calendar behind the register, same as yours.

He'd always ask me the week before, "Hey Harp, what's the birthday plan?"

And every year, I'd have to tell him...there is no plan.

Mom's at work.

Dad's who knows where.

So he'd take us to the diner.

MAEVE. And he'd always order way too much food.

HARPER. Yeah...

It was never weird to you that your dad always gave me the leftovers?

MAEVE. No?

HARPER. And ordered the extra burgers the exact way my brothers liked?

MAEVE. I guess I didn't –

HARPER. He was the reason I had birthdays.

I should've gone into the funeral.

(*Beat.*)

MAEVE. *(Jokingly.)* It might have been for the best.

I would've ripped your head off either way.

(They laugh.)

HARPER. Your dad taught me to pay attention…

When you kicked me out earlier, I sat in the diner, ordered a milkshake, and looked at the store across the street.

I remember people-watching with you and your dad over there as kids.

He knew everyone's name.

What food they liked, what food they hated.

I mean, he would talk to people at the registers for, like, hours.

It was almost impossible to buy ice.

Whatever was going on in your life, he stayed the same.

He was always there.

Honestly, your dad almost made me appreciate it here.

And I was sitting over there, after you went off on me.

And I watched all those people come into this old grocery store and they always left happier than they came.

It just made me miss this place.

And your dad.

And you.

MAEVE. Maybe you have to leave a place to miss it.

HARPER. I know I did.

It's funny, I don't know if I would've been able to leave without him.

MAEVE. What are you talking about?

HARPER. The letter.

MAEVE. What letter?

HARPER. The letter of recommendation your dad wrote?

The admissions people at school said it was a huge reason why I got the scholarship.

I was never able to thank him enough.

> (*Beat.* **MAEVE**'s *face falls.*)

Maeve, what's up?

MAEVE. Oh my god.

HARPER. What?

MAEVE. He didn't tell me.

HARPER. What do you mean he didn't tell you?

MAEVE. I mean he didn't tell me.

About the letter.

> (**MAEVE** *throws out her milkshake and goes back to work.*)

HARPER. I thought you knew.

MAEVE. Doesn't matter now, I guess.

He's gone –

HARPER. Maeve, whoa –

MAEVE. No.

He's really gone.

I can't even be mad at him anymore.

> (*But she can be mad at* **HARPER**.)

> (*The teens –* **DREW, BLAKE, JESSE,** *and* **JORDAN** *– slowly come in and witness the last few lines.*)

And it's been suuuper fun catching up with you.

But I'm not my dad.

I'm not going to pity you just to make you feel better.

And all the milkshakes in the world won't make me forget that.

>   (*A really uncomfortable beat.*)
>
>   (**HARPER** *is hurt. Shocked. Embarrassed.*)
>
>   (*After the rage dissipates,* **MAEVE** *realizes she pushed too far.*)

Harper, I didn't mean –

HARPER. I know what you meant.

Great catching up.

>   (**HARPER** *rushes out.*)
>
>   (**MAEVE** *is at the cash register.*)
>
>   (*The* **TEENS** *are uncomfortable.*)
>
>   (**JESSE** *tries to break the tension.*)

JESSE. (*Trying to small talk.*) Boy, the weather sure is…

JORDAN. – weather!

BLAKE. Nice save!

JORDAN. Thanks!

MAEVE. What do you guys want?

DREW. Well, we finished up the apples.

MAEVE. Did they make it in the dumpster?

>   (*Beat.*)

BLAKE. Define "in" –

(**DREW** *hits* **BLAKE.**)

BLAKE. OW.

DREW. Why did Harper run out?

MAEVE. Doesn't matter.

DREW. Seems like it kinda matters –

MAEVE. Okay, whatever.

You got rid of the apples. Can I do something else for you?

JESSE. We just thought since we did a job for you –

MAEVE. Oh, now you're employees?

JESSE. I mean technically!

DREW. You didn't want those rotten apples.

JORDAN. And we got rid of 'em for you.

BLAKE. *(Like a mobster.)* And you'll never hear from them again.

They're sleeping with the fishes.

JESSE. Blake, that was really good.

BLAKE. Thanks, my uncle let me watch *The Godfather*.

MAEVE. *(Over it.)* Alright.

What do you guys want?

DREW. Payment –

MAEVE. *(Laughing.)* I'm not paying you –

JORDAN. Not in money!

MAEVE. Then what?

DREW. Mentos.

Diet Coke.

Cinnamon.

Gallon of milk.

MAEVE. GUYS.

BLAKE. The cinnamon challenge.

The milk challenge.

And the Mentos and Diet Coke fountain.

JORDAN. *(Like the holy grail.)* The trifecta of parking lot chaos.

MAEVE. No way.

JESSE. Come on!

JORDAN. This is the only place we hang out.

> *(**MAEVE** is shocked by this.)*

MAEVE. Really?

DREW. Jesse and Jordan's parents both work.

Blake didn't make the soccer team so they have a bunch of free time.

And my weekends are open until the school play so… your dad always gave us a place to be dumb.

> *(**MAEVE** takes a moment.)*

MAEVE. Mentos and Diet Coke.

That's it.

DREW. DEAL.

> *(**DREW** spits in their hand before going to shake **MAEVE**'s.)*

MAEVE. I'm not touching your hand.

DREW. FAIR.

> *(All of the **TEENS** but **DREW** grab their supplies and rush out.)*
>
> *(As they leave, **MAEVE** half-heartedly yells.)*

MAEVE. Thank you for shopping.

> (**DREW** *is still there. They go up to* **MAEVE**.*)*

DREW. So, Harper –

MAEVE. How do you even know Harper?

DREW. She used to be in the store just as much as you were when I was younger.

My mom never wanted to go to your guys' register 'cause you were always talking to each other.

MAEVE. *(Laughs a bit.)* That makes sense.

DREW. And now you guys are fighting?

MAEVE. No. Yes?

I just feel like I'm saying all the wrong things.

It's been a day.

I don't know, Drew, just go... Go have fun in the parking lot.

DREW. Okay...

Just, maybe it's not about saying the right thing?

Maybe it's about hearing it?

> (**MAEVE** *thinks about this for a second. Smiles.*)

MAEVE. Yeah, thanks for the advice.

You're a child.

Go away.

DREW. I will but by my own choice.

(In the direction of the parking lot.) DON'T BLOW THINGS UP WITHOUT ME!

The Canned Goods Aisle 2

(**BILL** *returns to the canned goods aisle.*)

(*He catches sight of* **CRAIG** *in his episode of panic.*)

BILL. Whoa there, junior, you alright up there?

(**CRAIG** *closes his eyes tight in fear and shame.*)

CRAIG. Um, not doing so alright up here, sir.

BILL. You got a health condition or something?

You see a ghost?

CRAIG. No, not really…

BILL. This that nervous thing you talked about earlier?

You got a nerves problem?

CRAIG. Um, sort of?

Yeah.

Yeah I get nervous a lot.

But um this, this specifically, I think this specifically has more to do with my intense fear of heights.

BILL. Intense fear of heights?

CRAIG. Precisely yes.

BILL. Now why the heck did you try and work in a grocery store with a fear of heights?

CRAIG. I didn't know you guys had to reach so high!

BILL. You never walked through here and thought, "Huh, I better look up and appreciate all the stunning signage and upstocking the good people of this store do to finesse and beautify my shopping experience"?

CRAIG. Um, literally no, never.

BILL. Really?

CRAIG. I never looked up in the store.

I've been coming here all my life so I know what aisles are what and where on the rows to find things.

It never occurred to me that this job could be so dangerous!

BILL. Never looked up…

CRAIG. But you see the problem is I'm up here now and I'm looking down and I can't do it.

BILL. Upstock the beans?

CRAIG. No, not even that! I… I… I can't get down.

BILL. Well, just get down.

CRAIG. No it's not that easy for me!

BILL. Well, you can't stay up there forever, bucko.

CRAIG. Are you sure about that?

BILL. And you can't let fear dictate how you live your life!

CRAIG. Easy for you to say! You're like the toughest guy to ever work in a grocery store!

BILL. No, actually, I'm not.

CRAIG. You're not?

BILL. You wanna know why I started this job?

CRAIG. Yeah.

BILL. 'Cause I know about this nervous stuff you're talking about.

I had something like it too.

Something called "social anxiety."

CRAIG. Oh wow, yeah, that's a thing!

It's really tough on people.

BILL. Yeah, yeah.

Call it what you want.

All I know is how I felt…

> (**BILL** *takes a moment and remembers.*)

Like I couldn't even leave my house.

Like I couldn't hold a conversation.

Like it was totally taking over my life.

> (**BILL** *takes a step closer to* **CRAIG** *on the ladder.*)

CRAIG. That's so terrible.

BILL. I know.

It got so bad, my family started worrying about me.

Wondering how I was gonna get on if I couldn't even talk to people.

> (**BILL** *takes another step to the ladder.* **CRAIG** *doesn't notice.*)

CRAIG. Oh I know all about that.

And it's like, my worrying causes their worrying and I worry about that and then we're all caught up in this horrible, twisted worry-tornado.

> (**BILL** *takes the first step on the ladder toward* **CRAIG**, *very, very slowly.*)

BILL. So, you know what I did?

> (**CRAIG** *is fully mesmerized by the story and by feeling understood.*)

CRAIG. What did you do?

> (**BILL** *takes another step.*)

BILL. I got a job.

CRAIG. You did?

BILL. At this store.

> (**CRAIG** *unconsciously takes a step down toward* **BILL**.*)

CRAIG. Really?

> (**BILL** *goes up another step, meeting him one step below.*)

BILL. Yes. Started in the same position you're in now.

CRAIG. Unbelievable.

> (**BILL** *takes a step down.*)

BILL. And it helped!

> (**CRAIG** *follows him down another step, without realizing it.*)

CRAIG. Wait, really?!

BILL. Really.

Having a job where I can start my day in the quiet before open, just me and the shelves.

Then warm up my conversation skills with the early-bird shoppers.

Eventually, I became friends with my coworkers, and the owners.

And it got a lot easier to talk to people.

I got comfortable with it.

I can even talk to strangers now too.

> (**CRAIG** *follows him down another step.*)

CRAIG. Like me?

BILL. Well, I'd say you and me aren't strangers anymore. We're –

CRAIG. Friends?!

BILL. We're coworkers.

> (**CRAIG** *follows him down to the final step.*)

CRAIG. Does that mean you're gonna let me keep this job?

Even though I can't get off the ladder?

BILL. Look down, kid. You just did.

> (**CRAIG** *looks down; he's on the ground.*)

CRAIG. Oh my goodness!

How did you do that?!

BILL. Life can be scary sometimes.

Take it day by day, piece by piece.

CRAIG. Step by step!

BILL. And remember, it's easier if you don't do it alone.

CRAIG. So what do I do next?

If the ladder's out?

BILL. I say we keep you as close to the ground as we can get.

> (**BILL** *leaves and comes back with a super nice dust mop.*)
>
> (**CRAIG** *grabs it and hugs it with joy. It's his life preserver, his salvation.*)

CRAIG. Oh, thank you, thank you!

You won't regret this!

The floors will never be cleaner!

BILL. I trust you, kid.

And if you ever decide to take on the ladder again... have me spot you next time.

CRAIG. Deal.

BILL. Deal.

> (**CRAIG** *takes off down the aisle with his mop.* **BILL** *climbs the ladder with a box of beans to upstock. He takes in the view with pride.)*

The Bakery: Fixing a Cake

(Two women, **DIANA** *and* **LIV**, *come into the grocery store in bridesmaid dresses covered in cake.)*

*(***MAEVE*** is at the register and notices them.)*

MAEVE. Oh my gosh –

DIANA. I know, I know.

LIV. Do you guys have cakes?

MAEVE. Our baker is out for the day –

LIV. ARE YOU KIDDING ME –

MAEVE. Jeez –

DIANA. Liv!

(To **MAEVE.***)* Sorry, sorry.

It's been... Well, it's been a day.

Baking aisle?

MAEVE. Aisle 6.

You know what, let me get you some supplies.

Assuming you need something big –

LIV. YOU THINK?

DIANA. Liv!

(To **MAEVE.***)* Sorry, yes, anything you can find would be a lifesaver.

MAEVE. Let me see what I can do.

*(***MAEVE*** *walks off.)*

*(***LIV*** *starts hyperventilating.)*

*(***DIANA*** tries to calm her down.)*

DIANA. Liv, it's gonna be okay. Calm down –

LIV. Calm down?

CALM DOWN?

Di, I ruined the wedding.

Sadie is gonna kill me.

Adam is never gonna talk to me again.

I am literally so screwed, I shouldn't even go to the wedding –

DIANA. Sadie would kill you if you didn't show up, that's for sure.

LIV. Diana.

I destroyed the wedding cake –

DIANA. You didn't destroy the –

LIV. Really?

Because there are nine layers of vanilla cake spread across the reception hall.

Oh my god, when she sees that.

Sadie is gonna go berserk.

DIANA. Liv –

LIV. She's gonna take my dress away.

She can't. I love this dress.

I LOOK SO GOOD IN THIS DRESS.

DIANA. Liv –

LIV. And I love Sadie!

And Adam!

Oh my god, I suck.

I suck so hard.

I suck, suck, suck –

DIANA. Liv.

Breathe.

It's just a cake.

LIV. It's a *wedding* cake, Diana.

DIANA. It's egg, butter, and flour that creates some big monstrosity of sugar.

It's a cake.

Sadie might be sad; Adam might be annoyed.

But they'll understand.

They love you. They want you there.

LIV. But –

DIANA. No buts!

If we need to bake a cake, we bake a cake.

If we need to find another store, we'll drive to a different state.

Dude, I'll make a tower of gummy worms and cookies if I have too.

LIV. She does weirdly love cookie-gummy-worm sandwiches.

DIANA. SEE.

A bad friend wouldn't know about her obsession combining gummy worms and cookies!

LIV. I guess.

DIANA. And...

Okay, how about our trip to New York?

LIV. That was years ago –

DIANA. Not the point.

Do you remember it?

LIV. Yeah, it sucked.

We got scammed –

DIANA. We didn't get "scammed"!

We did a very…very expensive bus tour that was given by a person who clearly knew nothing about New York City.

LIV. Oh my god that was my idea.

Do you think Sadie is still mad about that?

DIANA. NO.

Because it sucked in the moment but that trip was monumental.

Remember the spitball you shot at the guys in front of us?

LIV. Yeah.

Got 'em clear in the back of the dome.

Thank god they thought it was funny.

DIANA. Those guys invited us out that night, and one of them had a high-school friend that was visiting town and tagged along…

That high-school friend was –

LIV. – Adam

I know, dude –

DIANA. NO, YOU DON'T GET TO THROW IT AWAY LIKE THAT.

LIVVY!

Sadie and Adam literally met because of you –

LIV. Because of a spitball I shot.

DIANA. Yeah.

You have really good aim.

LIV. *(Spiraling.)* That's good.

I should put that in my speech tonight.

If there was gonna be a wedding.

Which there isn't.

'Cause I ruined it.

And Sadie is gonna use her veil to choke me to death –

DIANA. Honestly I'm happy you dropped the cake.

LIV. Di.

That's dumb.

DIANA. No really!

We're her only bridesmaids.

Now, her cake, whatever it will be, is going to have some weird, insane, goofy story behind it.

LIV. I don't know –

DIANA. Because we WILL get a cake.

I don't care if I have to fight a guy for a cupcake.

I don't care if I have to make it out of mud.

I DON'T CARE IF I NEED TO BUY A CAKE OFF THE DARK WEB.

LIV. I don't think that's what that's for.

DIANA. WHATEVER.

We will have a cake.

It will probably be weird.

But it'll be okay because it'll be something we got FOR Sadie.

LIV. And it'll match perfectly with our cake-covered dresses.

>*(They laugh.)*

DIANA. It's gonna be okay.

Whatever happens –

MAEVE. *(Offstage.)* I found something!

DIANA. Oh thank god –

LIV. I thought you were excited about the adventure –

DIANA. Yeah, but like, we still need a cake.

>(**MAEVE** *rolls on a beautiful three-tier cake, each tier a different color.)*

>(**DIANA** *and* **LIV** *go wide-eyed.)*

LIV. How –

How –

How did you –

MAEVE. I told you that the baker is out today.

He sometimes makes cakes that don't sell so I had someone put three of the day-olds together.

I think it looks –

DIANA. It's perfect.

LIV. Almost.

>(**LIV** *grabs gummy worms and cookies that are hung at the cash register.)*

>(She opens them up and puts them all across the top of the cake.)*

MAEVE. Well, that's pretty weird –

DIANA. *(Almost crying.)* It's perfect.

(**DIANA** *and* **LIV** *hug.*)

LIV. Okay, how much do we owe you?

MAEVE. Nothing.

It's fine.

DIANA. No let us –

(**MAEVE** *looks at their dresses.*)

MAEVE. Looks like you might have some more fires to put out today.

Good luck.

Tell your friend I said congratulations.

(**DIANA** *and* **LIV** *hug* **MAEVE**.)

DIANA. Thank you.

LIV. And sorry for being a jerk.

MAEVE. All good.

(**DIANA** *and* **LIV** *run out with their new cake.*)

(**MAEVE** *looks at the door as they go.*)

(*Feels good about doing something thoughtful for these friends.*)

(*Thinks about* **HARPER**.)

The Dairy Aisle 3

(Even later that day.)

*(**BROOKE** is pacing up and down the dairy aisle, stealing occasional glances between the shelves of milk. Waiting.)*

*(**ANNA** enters, clutching her stomach.)*

BROOKE. Hey!

ANNA. Hey.

BROOKE. Well, how'd it go?

ANNA. Not so good.

BROOKE. Not in the bathroom, with the milkman!

The man behind the milk!

ANNA. No, I know… It was only okay.

BROOKE. Only okay?

ANNA. We made plans to meet back on the loading dock on his break like I told you.

BROOKE. Yes! So romantic!

Was it romantic?

Tell me everything.

ANNA. It was… I don't know.

It was sort of…anticlimactic, I guess?

BROOKE. Oh no.

ANNA. Yeah, like… I've been coming to this aisle and pretending to check for expiration dates and the best deals on cottage cheese for weeks now.

And I've been imagining what this day would be like, this day I'm brave enough to actually do something.

And I've had this picture in my head of how my life would change once we met, and I saw his face, and he saw mine.

But then in the end… / he was just some guy!

BROOKE. / He was just some guy.

ANNA. Yeah.

BROOKE. Yeah.

ANNA. I mean, he was nice and everything.

He told me about how the store deals with waste, and about dumpster diving, and like, what the rats out there like to eat…

BROOKE. Oooh yeah, super nice…

ANNA. But I guess he just couldn't live up to the picture in my head.

BROOKE. And what were you picturing? In your head? Of his head?

ANNA. I honestly couldn't even tell you.

I think maybe I was just bored.

And now my stomach hurts.

> (**BROOKE** *passes* **ANNA** *another bottle of Lactaid from her pocket.*)

How do you still have more of this?

BROOKE. I told you, there was a sale.

ANNA. Thanks.

BROOKE. And you're not.

ANNA. Not what?

BROOKE. Boring.

ANNA. You have to say that, you're my best friend!

BROOKE. I get to say that!

BROOKE. You're my best friend.

> *(They smile at each other, sitting now with their backs against the cases of milk.)*

I know you better than anyone else.

And not just the idea of you, not just the concept of some floating head behind the two percent.

But actual, real deal, entertaining, very lactose-intolerant you.

Could a boring person keep me this enthralled on a trip to the grocery store?

ANNA. Definitely not.

BROOKE. Absolutely not!

You don't need the man behind the milk.

And you don't need the milk!

Did you see the new selection of milk alternatives Maeve has stocked?

There's plenty of fish in the sea.

ANNA. Yes.

There are.

But only one best friend in the whole wide world.

And I'm lucky that you're mine.

BROOKE. Me too.

> *(**ANNA** and **BROOKE** begin to head down the aisle to leave the store.)*

> *(**BROOKE** stops, remembering something.)*

Did you see the new employee they brought in today?

ANNA. Why don't you show me?

> *(They link arms and exit happily.)*

The Registers 4

(**MAEVE** *is at the cash register.*)

(*It's the end of the day.*)

(*She's full of remorse, still angry, still hurt, still grieving.*)

(**DREW** *walks in without the other teens.*)

(*They look nervous, like they might be in trouble.*)

MAEVE. Well, Drew, how was causing havoc in my parking lot?

DREW. Uh, good.

MAEVE. Where's your friends?

DREW. What friends?

I have no friends.

I actually just moved to this town, we've never met, and my name is Dynamo.

MAEVE. Drew –

DREW. We might have done something...

And it was my idea...

And it might have been illegal...

MAEVE. ILLEGAL?

DREW. MIGHT HAVE BEEN ILLEGAL –

MAEVE. HOW DO YOU NOT KNOW?

DREW. I'm a kid!

I don't know laws!

MAEVE. What did you do?

DREW. I just –

I remember that you said you and Harper were having a tough time...

And she was gonna leave, so I thought maybe we should get her to stay!

MAEVE. Drew.

DREW. Maeve.

MAEVE. What. Did. You. Do.

DREW. *(Very quiet.)* We surrounded her car with Diet Coke bottles and created a –

MAEVE. SPEAK UP!

DREW. WE SURROUNDED HER CAR WITH DIET COKE AND CREATED A RUBE GOLDBERG MACHINE THAT BLEW UP THIRTY MENTOS SLASH COKE BOTTLES AND GOT ALL OVER HER CAR.

> **(MAEVE** *is wide-eyed.)*

If it helps...it looked awesome.

> **(MAEVE** *is still silent.)*

> **(DREW** *makes an awkward explosion noise with their mouth.)*

> **(HARPER** *walks in; she looks exhausted.)*

HARPER. Do you have any paper towels...

> *(An awkward beat.)*

DREW. I'm gonna go...

You're the best, Maeve, I'll see you tomorrow.

> **(DREW** *starts to walk out, but stops at* **HARPER**.*)*

I just wanna say, I don't know what happened to your car.

HARPER. I didn't say it was my car...

> *(Beat.)*

> *(**DREW** has said too much.)*

DREW. Uh...have a great night you two!

And stay safe!

I hear there are people making really awesome soda explosions all over town.

> *(**DREW** leaves.)*

> *(**MAEVE** starts laughing.)*

> *(**HARPER** doesn't.)*

> *(It's uncomfortable.)*

HARPER. Paper towels?

MAEVE. Same aisle as always.

> *(**HARPER** walks into the aisles.)*

> *(**MAEVE** is alone for a moment.)*

> *(**HARPER** comes back with paper towels.)*

HARPER. Are you the only register open?

MAEVE. We're about to close so –

> *(**HARPER** plops her paper towels in front of **MAEVE**.)*

Oh you don't have to –

HARPER. I'll buy 'em.

I don't need your pity, right?

MAEVE. Harp –

HARPER. I just need to wipe down my driver's seat and I can get out of your life again.

MAEVE. Oh...

HARPER. Yeah...my windows were down.

MAEVE. That sucks.

> *(Beat.)*

I am really sorry.

HARPER. Well, we pulled worse back in our day.

MAEVE. Remember when we would have / shopping cart races down the hill.

HARPER. / shopping cart races down the hill.

MAEVE. My dad told me he'd switch to baskets only if we ever tried that again.

HARPER. How were we supposed to know grocery carts went that fast?

> *(Beat.)*

MAEVE. Did your company put you up at a hotel?

HARPER. I'm staying at Mom's.

How does your night look?

MAEVE. You're looking at it.

Closing as always.

HARPER. Didn't you open?

MAEVE. What's new?

HARPER. You didn't want to take today off?

Of all days?

MAEVE. My house is full of extended family making casseroles and talking about him.

Working a double didn't seem all that bad.

HARPER. I get that.

MAEVE. Plus...

Never mind, it's too weird.

HARPER. Tell me.

MAEVE. Well, it...

It sort of feels like he's still here?

HARPER. In the store?

MAEVE. Yeah.

Doesn't it?

> (**HARPER** *closes her eyes and listens.*)

HARPER. Maybe.

Like in the hum of the lights or something.

Or the freezers.

MAEVE. I don't know.

He was just always here.

> (*Beat.*)

You know, one of those kids asked me if I lived here earlier? Like in the store?

He thought my dad was magic.

HARPER. That's amazing.

MAEVE. But honestly, sometimes it feels like that.

Dad and I...and you, spent so much time here.

HARPER. We really did.

HARPER. Sometimes it felt like we would never leave.

MAEVE. Some of us didn't.

HARPER. Okay, well, go with me.

If you did, what would you want?

MAEVE. I always thought I'd get out of here.

Go off to college...with you...

Then...

I don't know what.

I guess that's really what I wanted.

The freedom to figure it out.

HARPER. I always thought you'd be a great lawyer.

MAEVE. *(Laughing it off.)* What are you talking about?

HARPER. Really!

You were a killer on the debate team.

Plus you won like every argument with your dad.

MAEVE. That doesn't matter.

That's like so much school.

I have a two-year degree.

And it's like, a lot of work.

It's just not possible.

HARPER. Mae, you're tenacious.

Almost to a fault.

Nothing's impossible for you.

    (Beat.)

    (That meant so much to **MAEVE.***)*

    (And to **HARPER.***)*

MAEVE. I'm sorry –

HARPER. No, I'm sorry –

MAEVE. I love you.

This is so dumb –

HARPER. I LOVE YOU.

I'm so dumb!

HARPER & MAEVE. We're so dumb!

> (*The two hug real big.*)

> (*The air is finally cleared.*)

HARPER. You want to get out of here?

MAEVE. I do.

I just have to close up first –

> (**MAEVE** *starts closing.*)

> (**HARPER** *helps.*)

> (*They work together like no time has gone by.*)

> (**MAEVE** *remembers something.*)

Oh, wait.

It was so crappy of me to kick you out earlier.

I don't know what I wanna do with the store yet but I'll totally read your fancy-investor-boss-corporate-megamart contract.

HARPER. Yeah, well, actually –

MAEVE. Harp, it's fine.

Give it to me, I'll take a look!

> (**HARPER** *hands the envelope to* **MAEVE.**)

(As she reads, **HARPER** *explains.)*

HARPER. I know I left.

But I never stopped thinking about this place.

I made some money these past few years and learned a ton at my last internship with that investment company.

MAEVE. Megamart corporate overlords –

HARPER. *Investment company.*

I started figuring things out.

Including how to write contracts.

And make business plans.

MAEVE. Harp, what is this?

HARPER. It's a co-ownership agreement for the store.

You and me.

Mae and Harp.

Together again.

MAEVE. How would this even –

HARPER. I have all the business savvy from school.

You know this place like the back of your hand.

We'd be an unstoppable team.

MAEVE. I don't want you to get stuck here after you got out.

HARPER. It's not stuck.

It's my choice.

Say the word and I give my notice to those "corporate overlords."

I missed you so much and I wanna be friends again.

Partners.

MAEVE. That sounds incredible.

HARPER. Plus…it wouldn't have to all be on you anymore.

I'll be here, so you could leave.

You could stay.

You could go to school.

Hell, you could go to law school.

MAEVE. Grocery stores are a good business but we aren't making that kind of money –

HARPER. We will.

But, flip to the next page.

> (**MAEVE** *does.*)

> (*She's stunned.*)

MAEVE. No way.

HARPER. A business plan and a budget.

I even worked out a way to cover your tuition to get your bachelor's.

You're an investment, same as the store.

> (**MAEVE** *attack hugs* **HARPER.**)

MAEVE. You really don't have to do this.

HARPER. It's sort of the least I can do.

This place took care of me.

So did you.

I want to return the favor.

> (*Beat.*)

MAEVE. We're keeping the store in the family.

HARPER. And now we can get even faster shopping carts.

MAEVE. We need to celebrate.

I know you already had a couple, but, a best friend twist?

HARPER. I will literally never say no to milkshakes.

I'll lock up.

MAEVE. I'll grab the lights.

(**HARPER** *grabs the keys.*)

(**MAEVE** *goes to the lights by the front door.*)

(*We hear the hum of the store.*)

(*They smile at each other.*)

(**MAEVE** *turns off the lights.*)

(*Blackout.*)

End of Play

THE STOCKROOM

LIST OF SCENES

THE FOOD SAMPLES

Local teens Ollie and Kirby interact with Jules, a magical employee who gives out samples. A silly scene with a great spot to place a teacher or local celebrity in the show as Jules.

JULES – Male

OLLIE – Any gender

KIRBY – Any gender

MAEVE

THE CANDY AISLE

Toni is a babysitter helping the kid they watch, Randy, pick a type of candy to give out to their class. Randy learns about how food affects people in different ways.

TONI – Any gender

RANDY – Any gender

THE SNACK AISLE

A young mom and her teenage daughter talk about saving and splurging. Her daughter starts to understand saving and deciding between things that you need and things that you want.

SHELLY – Female

SHARON – Female

THE CEREAL AISLE

Ash is tasked by their mom to choose the cereal they want for breakfast. When their mom runs off to the car, Ash is confronted with this decision as all of the cereal mascots come to life around them.

SHEILA – Female

ASH – Any gender

COLONEL CRUNCH – Male

BOOM – Any gender

BAM – Any gender

BOW – Any gender

MARSHMALLOW MAN – Male

THE BREAK ROOM

Jamie and Dakota are both employees at the grocery store. They are reeling from a fresh breakup and are forced to have a conversation when they unfortunately run into each other in the break room.

DAKOTA – Any gender

JAMIE – Any gender

THE FLOWER SECTION

William, a hopeless romantic and store employee in the flower section, helps Samuel find flowers for his roommate. Throughout William's confusion with Samuel's relationship, Samuel teaches William the difference between platonic love and romantic love.

WILLIAM – Male

SAMUEL – Male

THE RESTROOMS

Four young hikers/adventurers stop by the store to use the public restroom in the midst of a multiday hike. The four friends discover why they are really on this hike and confront upcoming changes in their lives.

RIVER – Any gender

EZRA – Any gender

PARKER – Any gender

AVERY – Any gender

MAEVE

THE INTERCOM

Dale, Ronnie, and Kayla are working the registers as they ring up Rita. Rita becomes more and more confused as they use the intercom for communication seamlessly, but to Rita and the audience, the words that come through the store's speakers are muffled beyond recognition.

DALE – Male

RONNIE – Male

RITA – Female

KAYLA – Female

BILL – Male

THE CANNED GOODS AISLE
(ADDITIONAL TRANSITION SCENE)

A tableau and option for transitions using the characters from "The Canned Goods Aisle" scenes. Good use of comedy and clowning while the aisles are changing.

BILL

CRAIG

THE PRODUCE SECTION

Nance, a woman looking for love, has a conversation with Arthur, a grocery delivery man, about a recent Missed Connection. The two bond as the produce misters mist and Arthur helps Nance find her lost love.

NANCE – Female

ARTHUR – Male

The Food Samples: J'accuse

> (**JULES** *is an employee of the store who hands out samples. He has a mobile cart with popcorn chicken samples on it. He doesn't work on commission but one hundred percent acts like he does.*)

> (*He is an incredibly passionate and intense carnival barker.* **JULES** *is a great opportunity to cast a teacher or local celebrity in the show.*)

JULES. POPPPPPPPCORN CHICKEN!

GETCHA POPCORN CHICKEN HERE!

(**OLLIE** *and* **KIRBY** *walk on.*)

YOU THERE!

Are you interested in trying some sweet popcorn chicken?

KIRBY. *(To* **OLLIE***.)* Whoa, Ollie.

Check out this guy.

He's intense.

OLLIE. Right?

JULES. Well?!

May I interest either of you in some delectable popcorn chicken?

OLLIE. No thank you.

KIRBY. Yeah, we're good, guy.

JULES. Oh, it's quite alright.

We have many options, and I'm sure if you see something you like, I can get you a sample.

JULES. I'm sorta the "Big Cheese" around these parts! Too-da-loo!

> (**JULES** *exits with his cart.*)

KIRBY. Jeez, this guy!

OLLIE. I've never heard someone say "too-da-loo" not ironically.

KIRBY. He's like a carnival barker but in a grocery store.

OLLIE. Whatever.

Okay, Kirby, what did we need to get again?

KIRBY. People said barbecue and sour cream chips, Twizzlers, and oh!

I want that lemonade that they sell here.

It's amazing.

> (**JULES** *shoots on from the other side of the stage. He has a cart with lemonade samples.*)

JULES. LEMONADE!

SWEET, SWEET LEMONADE!

GETCHA LEMONADE HERE!

OLLIE. Whoa.

KIRBY. Is that the lemonade I like?

OLLIE. I think so –

JULES. Freshly squeezed and organic lemonade! The best lemonade in town!

Give it a try!

KIRBY. Uh, I'll take one.

JULES. Absolutely, my friend!

> (**KIRBY** *takes the lemonade. They drink it.*)

How's it taste?!

KIRBY. Uh...awesome.

OLLIE. *(To* **JULES***.)* Were you listening to us?

JULES. I beg your pardon?!

OLLIE. You heard us talking about the lemonade and put it on your cart? Weird move, guy –

JULES. I certainly did no such thing!

KIRBY. Yeah.

How'd you know about the lemonade?

JULES. I have NO clue what you speak of but I must be off! The sample man has much work to do!

Away!

    *(***JULES*** rushes off with his cart.)*

OLLIE. What a weird guy –

KIRBY. How'd he know?

OLLIE. He obviously was listening to us. Whatever.

KIRBY. It was just really fast.

OLLIE. I guess.

It's not like magic or something.

KIRBY. Yeah.

OLLIE. So chips, candy, OH.

Can we grab those little pretzel twists that have the powder on them?

KIRBY. Oh like the flavor-pretzel things?

OLLIE. Yeah, I love those little guys!

    *(***JULES*** comes on with a cart full of little pretzel samples.)*

JULES. PRETZELS!

OLLIE. Oh you gotta be kidding me.

JULES. PRETZEL SAMPLES!

SAMPLES OF LITTLE FLAVOR-PRETZEL THINGS!

KIRBY. That's what I called them!

JULES. ANY TAKERS ON THE PRETZELS –

OLLIE. HEY MAN.

STOP EAVESDROPPING.

JULES. Huh?!

KIRBY. YES.

J'ACCUSE.

J'ACCUSE ON YOU.

OLLIE.   EAVESDROPPING IS AN INVASION OF PRIVACY.

JULES. I'm confused.

Do either of you want a pretzel?!

KIRBY. Yeah, of course!

OLLIE. Obviously.

(They each take a pretzel and eat as they talk.)

But you can't buy us with your pretzels, weird uh –

*(***OLLIE*** *looks for a name tag.)*

JULES. Jules –

OLLIE. – weird JULES, the sample man!

JULES. I'm very sorry if I've done anything wrong but I'm just giving samples! I must be off but I'll see you both soon!

Thank you for shopping!

(**JULES** *rushes out.*)

(**OLLIE** *and* **KIRBY** *are really thrown off.*)

OLLIE. Okay, who is this guy?!

KIRBY. I don't know. It's insane.

He needs to be stopped.

OLLIE. Are we summoning him? Is he being summoned?

KIRBY. I don't know.

Say a food you like. Maybe he'll come back.

OLLIE. Uh, yeah. Okay.

(**OLLIE** *readies themselves like they are going to perform a séance.*)

I LIKE ICE CREAM SANDWICHES.

(*No one comes.*)

I LIKE BUBBLE GUM.

(*No one comes.*)

I LIKE PRETZELS –

(**MAEVE** *enters like a jump scare.*)

(**OLLIE** *and* **KIRBY** *leap out of their shoes.*)

MAEVE. Jeez, you two okay?

KIRBY. Do you work here?

MAEVE. I kinda own this place.

OLLIE. Okay, there's a guy –

KIRBY. A guy like (*Showing with their hands.*) this tall.

OLLIE. And he's like a wizard –

KIRBY. Or a warlock –

KIRBY. He might be a warlock!

MAEVE. What are you guys talking about?!

OLLIE. The sample man –

KIRBY. JULES.

HIS NAME IS JULES.

MAEVE. *(Tongue-in-cheek.)* Jules?

There is no one named Jules who works here!

(**KIRBY** *and* **OLLIE**'s *brains explode.*)

OLLIE.	KIRBY.
OH MY GODDDDDDD	WHAT IS HAPPENING.
DDDDDDDDDDDDDD.	WHO WAS THAT MAN.
HE WAS A WITCHHHH	WHO IS THAT GUY.
HHHHHHHHHHHHHH.	WHAT IS HAPPENING?!

MAEVE. AH.

NO.

SORRY.

I'M KIDDING.

OLLIE. REALLY?!

MAEVE. Yes!

Jeez, Jules works here. He's our sample guy.

He's not a witch or a warlock or a wizard. He's just very good at his job.

KIRBY. Thank god.

MAEVE. Here, let me help you guys find whatever you're looking for.

OLLIE. Ah.

Okay.

Thanks.

> (**MAEVE** *leads the two of them off. The stage is empty for a moment.*)

> (**JULES** *walks on with his cart one more time and crosses the stage as he yells.*)

JULES. ICE CREAM SANDWICHES!

BUBBLEGUM-FLAVORED ICE CREAM SANDWICHES!

BUBBLEGUM-FLAVORED ICE CREAM SANDWICHES WITH A SALTY PRETZEL CRUNCH!

GETCHA ICE CREAM SANDWICHES HERE!

> (**JULES** *walks offstage.*)

The Candy Aisle: Everything in Moderation

> (**TONI**, *a babysitter, is helping* **RANDY** *find something for everyone. They walk down the candy aisle and look at their options.*)

TONI. Okay, so what do we need?

RANDY. Treats.

TONI. Cool, what kind?

RANDY. Well, it's Daisy's birthday party. But Nathaniel can't eat nuts.

TONI. Got it, no nuts.

> (**TONI** *reaches for a bag of licorice.*)

How about these?

> (**RANDY** *consults a small scrap of paper.*)

RANDY. No, Jessica's mom doesn't like her to have any red dye 40.

TONI. Okayyy, well that rules out...half of the aisle. Anything else?

RANDY. Ari doesn't do gelatin.

TONI. Marshmallows are out then too...

RANDY. So maybe...

TONI. What?

RANDY. Never mind.

TONI. No really, what?

RANDY. Just that.

Just.

Well, I really like chocolate the best.

(**TONI** *smiles.*)

TONI. You got it boss, chocolate it is.

RANDY. But is that okay?

TONI. Of course it's okay, it's your month to buy birthday treats, isn't it?

RANDY. I guess.

TONI. What's up with you, kid? You love chocolate!

RANDY. But isn't it, you know, bad for you?

TONI. Well...

(**TONI** *thinks.*)

RANDY. You don't eat chocolate, do you?

TONI. That's different.

(**TONI** *pulls out a pump from their pocket used for type 1 diabetes.*)

(*Gesturing toward the pump.*) You see this guy?

Right now, I'm telling this little machine exactly what to do to keep the amount of sugar in my blood where it should be.

RANDY. I know, my mom explained it to me. It helps keep you healthy.

TONI. Exactly.

RANDY. And I'm not supposed to make comments on it. Or offer you too much dessert.

TONI. Well, I'm a grown-up, so I can handle those questions. And a little dessert.

RANDY. You can?

TONI. Yeah!

You see all this stuff on the shelves?

RANDY. Uh-huh.

TONI. Well, that stuff can help keep me healthy too, like, if my blood sugar is too low.

RANDY. The sugar can help you?!

TONI. Yeah, sometimes!

When it needs to, and in moderation.

But you don't need to think about that stuff, okay?

RANDY. Then why does my mom think about it?

TONI. What do you mean?

RANDY. My mom always says, *(Doing an impression.)* "A moment on the lips, forever on the hips."

TONI. Oh.

RANDY. Is that true?

TONI. Hmm.

Let me think about that for a second.

> **(TONI** *takes a beat to consider how to navigate this.)*

Okay, so it's like this. Your mom loves you, right?

RANDY. Yes.

TONI. And she has rules sometimes, to keep you healthy and safe, yeah?

RANDY. Yeah...

TONI. Like how much time you can spend with your screens, or how far down the street you can ride your bike?

RANDY. Uh-huh...

TONI. Well some rules about food are to help keep you safe too. Like me with sugar and Nathaniel with his peanuts!

RANDY. Then who's making the rules to keep Mom safe?

TONI. Um... Well I guess part of being an adult and growing up is figuring out those things for yourself.

Making the lifestyle you want.

You have to be your own mom at some point.

RANDY. That sounds terrible.

TONI. I know.

It kind of is sometimes.

But that's not something you have to worry about yet.

RANDY. So I can have chocolate?

TONI. Yeah, a little chocolate is fine.

Do you think your classmates will like it too?

RANDY. I think so!

I've seen them like it on Halloween and Valentine's Day too.

TONI. Then chocolate it is.

RANDY. Maybe after this aisle, we can get some healthy stuff too.

Marissa doesn't always get her lunch packed so she might want more than chocolate.

TONI. Oh yeah?

RANDY. Yeah.

Sometimes she has to eat the cheese sandwich they give you. It looks pretty yucky.

TONI. I think we can work on that.

> *(Beat.)*

You pay attention to other people a lot, don't you?

RANDY. Yeah

TONI. That's really nice of you.

RANDY. I just think everybody should get to be full.

TONI. Me too.

RANDY. Oh, and Stevie will need a treat too.

TONI. Alright then, and what does Stevie eat?

RANDY. Maybe bones?

TONI. Come again?

RANDY. Stevie is Conner's service animal.

I think he's the only one who doesn't do chocolate.

TONI. Got it.

We'll head to the pet food aisle next.

RANDY. Okay.

Thanks, Toni.

You're good at explaining things.

TONI. Anytime, kid.

(They exit.)

The Snack Aisle: A Treat

(A daughter, **SHELLY**, *and mother,* **SHARON**, *walk down an aisle. The mother is a young mom and the daughter is in her early teens.* **SHELLY** *is very excited and speaking at a mile a minute and her mother is stressed, tired, and just trying to finish her shopping list.)*

SHELLY. – an A on my Spanish test –

SHARON. – Shelly / I know –

SHELLY. – an A+ on my math quiz and I got the extra-credit answer on the Pythagorean theorem –

SHARON. And all of that is / wonderful but –

SHELLY. I placed fourth in OI at the speech tournament last weekend and I know, twelfth in cross country isn't my best, but please can you / just –

SHARON. SHELLY. I'm not gonna get you a ticket to the concert –

SHELLY. SHARON –

SHARON. Sharon?!

SHELLY. Sorry. Mom. Mom?

Mom, please.

SHARON. Shelly, there is no world where I am getting you tickets to the Holiday Ball –

SHELLY. But Mom!

SHARON. No buts –

SHELLY. Literally all my friends are going!

It's done by eleven, and everyone I love will be there. EVERYONE.

Jinx 9!

SHELLY. The Belle Boyz.

TAYLOR IS HEADLINING.

Mom, we have the money? Why can't / we just –

SHARON. WE have the money?

No, your dad and I have the money.

If you had the money, this wouldn't be a question –

SHELLY. But I can't work yet!

That's unfair, if I could work I would –

SHARON. *(Sarcastically.)* Oh, you would?

SHELLY. I WOULD.

You know I would.

If there weren't laws holding me back from the workforce, I'd be a millionaire!

SHARON. Come on –

SHELLY. It's true.

I would start at that popcorn shop. Mr. Larry's on Main?

And I'd work there for a while and then do like...a corporate takeover or something.

SHARON. You have no idea what that means.

SHELLY. ...no, I don't.

But the point is the WORLD is holding me back from being rich and buying my own ticket so as my mother...

(Sucking up.) ...and my absolute best friend in the whole world...you kinda have to buy me this ticket.

SHARON. *(Laughing.)* I don't have to do anything!

SHELLY. This is bull.

SHARON. Shell.

SHELLY. It is!

You and Dad never buy me anything.

You even made me put the $200 Grandpa got me in a...mutual fund?

SHARON. It's a savings account –

SHELLY. WHATEVER.

It's not in my pocket so please...MONEY.

SHARON. SHELLY –

SHELLY. I'm kidding!

Kinda.

SHARON. Your father and I get you everything you need!

SHELLY. Okay, well...

(**SHELLY** *grabs a box of cookies off the wall.*)

Can I have this?

SHARON. Do you like it?

SHELLY. *(Has never seen it before.)* Uh, yes.

Yes, it's my favorite.

SHARON. Alright, then –

SHELLY. So I can have this but I can't go to the concert?!

SHARON. *(Takes a breath.)* Okay.

This?

This is food?

Food, water, shelter, I'll always get you.

But if I get you everything you wanted then I couldn't afford the stuff you needed.

I couldn't get you these *(Looks at box.)* wildly sugary cookies.

SHARON. We all make sacrifices.

SHELLY. It feels like I'M making the sacrifice in this –

> (**SHARON** *lets out an exasperated sigh. She sits on the ground.*)

> (*This is super out of character;* **SHELLY**'*s confused.*)

Uh, Mom.

You can't sit on the ground. We're in public.

> (**SHARON** *holds out her phone.*)

> (*It's a flip phone.*)

Your phone, what about it?

SHARON. You don't think I want something nicer than this?

SHELLY. You always said –

SHARON. Shelly, it's from the early 2000s.

The four button is broken and it shocks me every time I call your father.

SHELLY. Jeez, really?

SHARON. Of course I want a nice phone.

I wanna be able to listen to the Ball Boyz –

SHELLY. The Belle Boyz –

SHARON. Or watch the new Janx 5 music video –

SHELLY. Jinx and it's nine –

SHARON. Whatever!

Come here.

> (**SHARON** *pulls* **SHELLY** *down on the ground.*)

(They both sit next to each other, leaning.)

We all want.

I *want*, your dad *wants*, you *want*.

My goal your whole life has been to make sure you have what you need –

SHELLY. And you have done that.

SHARON. NO DUH.

(They laugh.)

You're here, with me.

You are a wonderful girl.

I love you very much.

You gotta trust me when it comes to this stuff.

SHELLY. Fine.

SHARON. But I'll make you a deal.

If you take out the trash every day, do some chores for me, and mow Mr. Putnam's grass next door –

I will go halfsies with you on the ticket.

SHELLY. DEAL.

*(**SHARON** starts to walk out)*

*(**SHELLY** grabs the cookies from her mom and puts them back on the shelf.)*

SHARON. Shelly, why –

SHELLY. No, it's all good, Mom!

I don't need it!

*(**SHELLY** skips off)*

*(Her **MOM** follows, proud she got through to her.)*

The Cereal Aisle: Choices, Choices, Choices

(A mom, **SHEILA***, and her teenage kid,* **ASH***, walk into the cereal aisle.)*

ASH. This.

Is.

Torture.

SHEILA. You're almost done!

And hey, we're at your favorite aisle!

ASH. Wait, so can I?

SHEILA. What do you want?

You braved the treacherous journey of accompanying your mom grocery shopping. You get to pick the cereal for the week.

*(***ASH*** goes wide-eyed as they inspect all the colorful boxes.)*

(A voice comes on over the intercom.)

VOICE. Will the owner of a silver Honda please head to the parking lot. You left your car on.

SHEILA. Oh my gosh.

I have to go.

Give me a minute, sweetheart. Pick a cereal!

*(***SHEILA*** rushes out.)*

*(***ASH*** goes back to looking at the cereals.)*

(One of the boxes on the wall moves a little.)

(What was that?)

(Maybe they're seeing things.)

*(**ASH** goes back to looking at the boxes.)*

(Another one moves a bit more.)

*(**ASH** knows they saw something.)*

(But no one else is in the aisle.)

(They have to be seeing things.)

*(**ASH** goes back to looking at the cereal.)*

(One of the boxes jumps off the shelf and onto the floor.)

*(**ASH** rushes over and picks it up.)*

(It's a box of Colonel Crunch.)

*(Just as **ASH** goes to put it back, they hear a stern voice come from offstage.)*

COLONEL. A-ten-Hut!

*(**ASH** is startled and drops the box.)*

*(Just then, the cereal mascot **COLONEL CRUNCH** appears from smoke in the aisle.)*

WELL.

PICK UP MY BOX.

*(**ASH** does.)*

ASH. Uh, who are you?

COLONEL. I'm Colonel Crunch!

First Mate of the SS Fruit and commander of the Crunchy Battalion!

ASH. Like…

From the box?

COLONEL. Yes, Ash.

From the box.

ASH. How do you know my name?

COLONEL. Because I'm here to help you pick the best cereal!

ASH. But I don't know what to pick!

COLONEL. You get to choose for the whole family?

ASH. Yeah.

It's kinda a lot of pressure.

COLONEL. It can be!

ASH. Right?!

COLONEL. Well, if you're picking the best-tasting cereal, the decision is simple.

Colonel Crunch has real fruit flavor, is gluten-free, and has a satisfying crunch that will leave you full and ready to take on the day!

My cereal is by far the best choice, so why don't you just –

BOOM. *(Offstage.)* NOT.

BAM. *(Offstage.)* SO.

BOW. *(Offstage.)* FAST.

COLONEL. Oh not these numbskulls.

> *(Through another cloud of smoke, **BOOM**, **BAM**, and **BOW** enter the aisle. They are three **SIBLINGS** and are wearing shirts with their names on it.)*

BOOM. YOU.

BAM. DON'T.

BOW. WANT.

BOOM. COLONEL'S.

BAM. GARBAGE.

ASH. Is that –

COLONEL. The Krisper Kids.

Boom, Bam, Bow.

BOW. WE.

BOOM. MEET.

BAM. AGAIN.

BOW. COLONEL.

ASH. *(To* **COLONEL**.*)* Do they always talk like this?

COLONEL. No, they just –

Will you three knock it off?!

You're freaking out the kid.

BOOM. Fine.

But you aren't gonna get this sale, Crunch!

BOW. *(To* **ASH**.*)* Kid, picture it now.

BAM. A bowl.

Some milk.

A spoon.

And the crackling of thousands of little krispy bits of goodness.

> *(**BOOM** makes the crackling sound with their mouth.)*

COLONEL. Yeah, but what they don't tell you is they are only good if they are slathered in sugar.

BOW. That's not true!

BAM. You can eat us plain.

We just taste...like...

BOOM. Paper!

BOW. YEAH. PAPER.

BAM. *(To* **COLONEL**.*)* WE TASTE LIKE PAPER.

Take that, Colonel.

(The three siblings do some sort of handshake.)

ASH. I'm sorry, there's a lot going on. I'm kinda overwhelmed.

MARSHMALLOW MAN. *(Offstage.)* DID SOMEONE SAY MARSHMALLOW MAN?!

COLONEL. Literally no.

*(***MARSHMALLOW MAN*** flies onstage through smoke. He's a superhero.)*

MARSHMALLOW MAN. Hello, young child.

Pick me.

Marshmallow Man Cereal has sweet oat circles and is surrounded by super marshmallows.

COLONEL. They're not "super marshmallows."

They're just little marshmallows with your face on them.

MARSHMALLOW MAN. The perfect treat.

BOOM. YOU'LL.

BAM. NEVER.

BOW. WIN.

BOOM, BAM & BOW. Marshmallow Man!

COLONEL. Guys!

BOOM, BAM & BOW. Sorry.

MARSHMALLOW MAN. *(To* **ASH.***)* Pick me.

ASH. I –

MARSHMALLOW MAN. Pick me.

ASH. I don't –

MARSHMALLOW MAN. *(Trying to use mind control.)* PICK MEEEEEEEEEE!

ASH. *(To* **COLONEL.***)* What's he doing?

COLONEL. He's trying to control your mind. Marsh, cut it out.

You don't actually have powers.

MARSHMALLOW MAN. Yes I do.

> **(MARSHMALLOW MAN** *grabs his box off the wall. He reads from it.)*

"Marshmallow Man is the strongest hero in Puffball City, and if you eat his cereal, you can be just like him!"

See kid, pick me, be a hero.

COLONEL. That's a cereal box!

Will you all just leave the kid alone?!

BOOM. HE.

BAM. JUST.

BOW. WANTS.

BOOM. THE.

BAM. SALE.

BOW. FOR.

BOOM. HIMSELF –

COLONEL. WILL YOU THREE CUT THAT OUT!

I don't.

ASH. You don't?

COLONEL. I –

(*He gets down to* **ASH**'s *level.*)

Of course I want you to buy my cereal.

But making a decision for your whole family can be really overwhelming.

ASH. RIGHT?!

COLONEL. Take your time, look at the boxes, and think about what would make breakfast the best this week.

You have a lot to chew on.

It's your job to make sure your siblings, your mom, and your dad have a good morning!

Don't listen to us.

We're just cereal mascots.

ASH. Thanks.

COLONEL. Let's go, everyone!

MARSHMALLOW MAN. Wait, I wasn't –

COLONEL. NOW.

MARSHMALLOW MAN. Aw, man.

(**BOOM, BAM,** *and* **BOW** *all rush off through the smoke.*)

(**MARSHMALLOW MAN** *follows suit.*)

(*The* **COLONEL** *heads to the exit.*)

COLONEL. Good luck, kid.

Remember, nothing is more important…than a well-balanced breakfast.

*(The **COLONEL** hops through the smoke.)*

*(The smoke fades away and **SHEILA** rushes back on.)*

SHEILA. Well, we're all good.

The car wasn't stolen.

You make a decision yet, kid?

ASH. Uh, yeah.

I think so.

SHEILA. Great, what's for breakfast?

*(**ASH** goes to the wall.)*

(They take a moment and look over their choices.)

*(**ASH** grabs Colonel Crunch.)*

Ah, the old colonel.

A classic.

ASH. Yeah, I was really sold on it.

SHEILA. Well, let's keep going. Next is the frozen section!

*(**SHEILA** walks out.)*

*(**ASH** starts to as well, but they hear a noise; it's another box of Colonel Crunch falling off the shelf.)*

*(The **COLONEL** is watching.)*

(He's proud.)

*(**ASH** holds the box tight and walks out.)*

The Break Room: Extra Hours

(**DAKOTA**, *an employee at the store, is sitting at a table in the break room. They are alone and eating a sandwich.*)

(*The break room is basic.*)

(*Tables, counter, punch clock, some lockers.*)

(*After a few moments, **JAMIE**, a fellow employee wearing a backpack, walks in to punch their card.*)

DAKOTA. No.

JAMIE. Okay, give me a second to explain.

DAKOTA. Noooooooooooope.

Leave.

JAMIE. I picked up a shift.

DAKOTA. WHAT?

JAMIE. I know, but –

DAKOTA. ODD-NUMBERED DAYS ARE MINE.

JAMIE. DAKOTA, I KNOW.

DAKOTA. Do you, Jamie?

Do. You.

Because if I pull out my phone *(They do.)* and look at the calendar... *(They do.)*

OH, WOW.

IT'S A FREAKING ODD-NUMBERED DAY.

JAMIE. Brian is late on rent.

Okay?

DAKOTA. Why do I care if our – YOUR roommate is late on rent?

JAMIE. Because, I'm helping him out. Just…just let me work for today.

I will sync up our schedules next week and you will never see me again.

(*A long, uncomfortable beat.*)

DAKOTA. Fine –

JAMIE. THANK YOU.

DAKOTA. But not again.

Seeing you sucks.

JAMIE. Okay. Sorry. Thank you.

(*Beat.*)

My shift doesn't start for like five minutes and this is kinda the only place with service in the store.

Can I –

DAKOTA. Whatever.

Sit where you want.

(*Beat.*)

JAMIE.	**DAKOTA.**
Oh by the way –	And can you make sure –

DAKOTA. Oh, sorry.

JAMIE. No, uh –

DAKOTA. I was gonna say, can you just make sure Maeve doesn't put us in the same department.

I'm in produce so, like, work in something else.

I don't know.

JAMIE. Yeah.

For sure.

DAKOTA. What were you gonna say?

(**JAMIE** *remembers.*)

(*They pull a hoodie and a note out of their backpack.*)

(**DAKOTA** *goes a little wide-eyed.*)

JAMIE. I...

I didn't know you were working so I was gonna toss this in your locker.

Haven't seen you since last week when you set all these boundaries but I thought you'd want your favorite hoodie back.

DAKOTA. Uh –

Yeah, okay, cool.

JAMIE. And I changed our Mr. Tasty meal subscription to your mom's house so you can get those.

DAKOTA. You didn't have to –

JAMIE. You always liked them more than me.

(*Beat.*)

(**DAKOTA** *picks up the letter.*)

DAKOTA. And the –

JAMIE. Yeah.

Yeah, no.

Just, I just thought there were a few things I didn't get to say before you broke up –

DAKOTA. It was mutual.

JAMIE. I mean –

DAKOTA. You wanted to too –

JAMIE. No.

Yeah, no, I just meant like, it happened kinda fast.

I felt like I didn't get to say everything and before I knew it you moved out and changed our work schedules –

Which I'm totally fine with and completely understand.

I just, I just want to be able to say everything I think I need to, for closure or whatever.

DAKOTA. Okay...

Cool.

JAMIE. Uh, yeah.

I was just gonna toss it in your locker so...

    (**JAMIE** *gets up from the table and puts the letter in Dakota's locker.*)

DAKOTA. You can just give it to me –

JAMIE. Oh, jeez, no way.

You can't read that in front of me.

I'll die.

Just, uh, maybe read it after you leave. So like –

DAKOTA. I still have two hours.

Just on a ten.

JAMIE. Cool.

So then.

Cool.

    (*A long uncomfortable beat.*)

(They exchange glances; they look at their phones.)

(It kinda sucks.)

JAMIE. *(So awkwardly.)* Yikes.

DAKOTA. Yup.

This is weird.

JAMIE. Never thought it would be like this.

DAKOTA. What are you talking about?

JAMIE. Well, this is my first breakup.

DAKOTA. Wha–

Oh my god it is.

I never clocked that.

JAMIE. You and Cameron Bettlemaker in the fourth grade.

DAKOTA. So you learned breaking hearts at a young age.

JAMIE. Come on.

I just…

I kinda thought it would be like a TV show.

DAKOTA. What are you talking about?

JAMIE. Whenever people break up in TV shows, I feel like one of two things happen.

Either it's huge and bad and toxic.

People scream, throw expensive vases, maybe curse each other out and then do some more damage to their ex's stuff.

OR it's really sad, and everyone is crying and snotting and stuff, and then like two hours later, they run back into each other's arms.

We, like, didn't do that.

DAKOTA. *(Realizing.)* Yeah, I guess not.

JAMIE. We just like...decided.

Made a choice.

I don't know.

DAKOTA. Are you disappointed I didn't break more stuff?

JAMIE. NO!

No, I just...

I thought I'd feel more in the moment.

Instead, I just have felt kinda weird for the last week.

Maybe empty?

Maybe sad?

Maybe just different.

I don't know.

> *(Jamie's phone goes off.)*

> *(It's a WAY too loud and annoying alarm.)*

That's my alarm.

DAKOTA. I know.

That's one thing I will not miss.

That insane alarm.

JAMIE. What will you miss?

> **(DAKOTA** *is stunned.)*

> **(JAMIE** *takes it back.)*

I'm just kidding.

I am...

Sorry.

Uh, okay, I'll go tell Maeve I'm here and request "not produce."

(**JAMIE** *starts out.*)

(*They stop.*)

JAMIE. Oh, and, seriously, (*References the locker.*) don't open it till you leave, cool?

DAKOTA. For sure.

JAMIE. Thanks.

Have a good shift, Dakota.

DAKOTA. You too, Jamie.

(**JAMIE** *leaves.*)

(**DAKOTA** *immediately goes to the door and makes sure* **JAMIE** *left fully.*)

(*They go to their locker and grab the letter.*)

(*They take a moment, and of course, open the letter.*)

(*They read.*)

(*They read.*)

(*They read.*)

(*Things hit them for the first time.*)

(*Feels weird.*)

(*Maybe empty?*)

(*Maybe sad?*)

(*Maybe just different.*)

(*They sit back down.*)

The Flower Section: Coming up Roses

> (**WILLIAM**, *an employee and hopeless romantic, is working in the flower section of the store.*)

> (**SAMUEL**, *a young man, comes over and begins looking at flowers.*)

WILLIAM. Well hello, sir.

SAMUEL. Hey man, I'm fine.

WILLIAM. Alright.

> *(Beat.)*

Well, if you need any help, let me know.

SAMUEL. Got it.

> *(Beat.)*

WILLIAM. You getting flowers for a lady?

SAMUEL. Uh, yeah, I guess.

WILLIAM. That's great.

Very chivalrous of you!

I have to recommend the lovers' bundle, I could even wrap it in some of our heart plastic –

SAMUEL. Oh god, no.

No, she's uh –

No, not like that.

WILLIAM. What do you mean?

SAMUEL. Just friends.

We're just friends.

WILLIAM. You're...

You're uh –

SAMUEL. *(Seeing his name tag.)* Okay, uh, William?

WILLIAM. Yes. *(Points at name tag.)* William.

SAMUEL. Great.

William, my name is Samuel.

And I'm getting flowers for my female best friend, Lucy.

So, that's what is happening.

> (**WILLIAM** *is kinda short-circuiting.*)

WILLIAM. Uh –

SAMUEL. I really don't need any help. Thank you.

WILLIAM. O...kay.

> *(Beat.)*

> (**WILLIAM** *clearly is holding in many questions.)*

> (**SAMUEL** *recognizes this, rolls his eyes, and gives in.)*

SAMUEL. Is everything okay, William?

WILLIAM. It's just...you and a –

SAMUEL. Girl. A girl is my friend.

Not that weird.

WILLIAM. But you love her, right?

SAMUEL. What?!

WILLIAM. You're harboring love for her?

Like secret love deep, deep down?

And she loves you?

And you're going to admit it to her?

Hence, the flowers?

SAMUEL. I'm getting flowers for her because she likes fresh flowers in the apartment when she gets up and she has a big interview tomorrow.

WILLIAM. Apartment?

SAMUEL. Yeah, our apartment?

WILLIAM. *(Too loud.)* YOU LIVE TOGETHER?!

SAMUEL. YEAH.

JEEZ.

We're roommates!

WILLIAM. I'm sorry to tell you this.

You love Lucy.

No way around it.

Give her a call and I want to watch.

(**SAMUEL** *is so annoyed and confused.*)

SAMUEL. No, look, dude, I don't love Lucy like that.

She's a platonic friend.

And I'm not going to call her because she is on a date with her boyfriend –

WILLIAM. *(Thinks he gets it.)* OH?

Ohhhhhhhh.

I get it now.

SAMUEL. Do you?

WILLIAM. YES.

Yes, I do.

I get it.

SAMUEL. Uh okay, man.

(**SAMUEL** *goes back to shopping.*)

WILLIAM. You CAN'T love her because she loves someone else –

SAMUEL. DUDE.

WILLIAM. No, it makes sense.

She has a boyfriend and you don't want to break them up.

She's happy and your love for her goes so much deeper than just romantic so you can't ruin that for her –

SAMUEL. NO.

WILLIAM. – so you have to tuck your love deep, deep down until she is open to it.

You guys have probably never been on the same page with your love but it's always been bubbling.

It's always been there.

It's just there and waiting to erupt like a love volcano.

SAMUEL. Man, no.

No.

Not at all –

WILLIAM. You probably don't even know you love her.

SAMUEL. *(Annoyed.)* Now, how would that work?

WILLIAM. Your whole lives, you and Lucy have always been side by side. Best friends.

It's always been Samuel and Lucy. Sam and Lu–

SAMUEL. No one calls me Sam.

WILLIAM. – and being friends for so long has created a friendship, a trust, a bond that is unbreakable.

But as you both grew, and learned, you slowly fell in deep, deep, passionate love with each other –

SAMUEL. Gross.

WILLIAM. – but you could never do anything about it!

She's your best friend!

You're her confidant.

And over years and years of love refusing to surface, you each have gotten to your respective breaking points, but the other one was never in the right place.

They were doing a semester abroad or had some partner you just couldn't stand, but you couldn't say that!

You couldn't say anything.

So you sat.

You sat and you waited and you got to a point, Sam.

SAMUEL. Again, no one calls me Sam.

WILLIAM. You got to a point where you just couldn't do it anymore.

So here you are.

Ready to buy flowers, the day before Lucy's big interview, to tell the love of your life… *(As Samuel.)* "Good luck, beautiful. Me? I don't need luck. I got my lucky charm right here."

And then dip, kiss, dating for three years, marriage, a few kids, a dog, a rocky year, couples therapy, makes you stronger, one more kid, buy a farm and grow lavender side by side 'til you both die in side-by-side grave plots where the tombstones are two huge rock arms holding hands.

Samuel and Lucy.

Holding hands forever.

> **(WILLIAM** *is tearing up.)*

> **(SAMUEL** *is shocked.)*

WILLIAM. Okay.

How close am I?

Don't worry.

You can tell me, Sam –

SAMUEL. NOT SAM.

Samuel.

My name is SAMUEL.

And dude, I don't know who you are, but I promise you, Lucy and I are just friends.

I love her LIKE A SISTER.

Her and Toby are wonderful together and I'm in a fantasy baseball league with him.

I'm just getting flowers because she likes them and honestly I do too.

They smell nice.

That's it.

Just two platonic friends of the opposite gender.

Nothing else to it.

WILLIAM. *(So let down.)* Oh.

SAMUEL. Yeah, sorry to ruin your rom-com, dude.

But, no, not in love.

Friend flowers.

> *(Beat.)*

> (**WILLIAM** *is really let down.*)

> (**SAMUEL** *realizes this, rolls his eyes, and unfortunately, feels obligated to fix it.)*

But uh…

I have been talking to this girl –

WILLIAM. REALLY?!

SAMUEL. DIFFERENT GIRL.

VERY DIFFERENT GIRL.

A girl from work.

She's nice and maybe she might like flowers too so…I guess I will get some for her as well –

WILLIAM. AND –

SAMUEL. But no heart plastic around them!

We have gone on, like, one date.

WILLIAM. But…love?

Heart means love –

SAMUEL. Come on, man, I'm throwing you a bone.

I'll get these sunflowers for my FRIEND Lucy. And let me get those roses for the girl from work –

WILLIAM. Roses are pretty romantic.

SAMUEL. William –

WILLIAM. Roses coming up!

> (**WILLIAM** *proudly packages the roses and gives them to* **SAMUEL**.)

Thank you for shopping!

SAMUEL. Yeah.

Thanks man.

> (**SAMUEL** *walks out.*)

> (**WILLIAM** *leans on the flower counter and puts his head in his hands.*)

WILLIAM. *(So lovey-dovey.)* Well, William, you did it again.

You made love happen.

Good job, William.

Good job.

The Restrooms: Hiking up a Mountain of Friendship

(*A young hiker and adventurer,* **RIVER**, *looks like they just got off the trail.*)

(*They're a leader; they're strong; they're proud.*)

(*They're looking at their fancy hiking watch.*)

(**RIVER** *found the one solo bathroom.*)

RIVER. Bathroom, located! Schedule, BEHIND. LET'S GO, SLOWPOKES!

(*Three other young people,* **PARKER**, **AVERY**, *and* **EZRA,** *walk in, exasperated and out of breath.*)

(*They look dead.*)

EZRA. (*So out of breath.*) ...water. I need water. I need water –

RIVER. (*Looking through the whole store with one sweep.*) It looks liiiiiiiiiiiiike Aisle 7.

EZRA. Great.

(**EZRA** *goes to rush off.*)

RIVER. But electrolytes are in Aisle 4. Probably better.

EZRA. Fine.

RIVER. And grab me a lemon one.

AVERY. And get me a strawberry.

PARKER. Oh and get me a kiwi and a melon –

AVERY. Do you need two?

PARKER. I like to mix them.

EZRA. (*Annoyed.*) It's fine.

EZRA. I have six hands so IT'S FINE.

RIVER. *(Too excited.)* Okay.

To stay on schedule, we all get two minutes in the bathroom!

That's exciting!

> (**AVERY** *and* **PARKER** *feign excitement.*)

Guys.

We have six more miles before camp.

This is the last stopping spot today so…

Pee, Pee, PEE!

> (**AVERY** *and* **PARKER** *look so tired.*)

PARKER. Whatever.

I'll pee.

Better than the woods.

> (**PARKER** *goes into the bathroom.*)

> (**AVERY** *sits on the floor.*)

> (**RIVER** *starts to high-step in place.*)

AVERY. River.

Don't you wanna take a break or something?

RIVER. Avery, I know that this your first long-distance, multiday hike-a-thon but I've been doing these for a while and you gotta keep your heart rate up if you wanna survive.

AVERY. Survive?!

RIVER. Live.

Make it.

Nothing is given to you in life, Avery. NOTHING.

(Beat.)

AVERY. You know, I know you grew up a survivalist and everything but I didn't realize how intense your family was 'til today.

RIVER. We're not intense.

AVERY. River.

Your siblings names are Forest, Sky, and Tree.

RIVER. Those are normal names.

AVERY. Your bedroom doesn't have a roof.

RIVER. It's called an "open-air skylight."

AVERY. The way you keep your house heated is a wood-burning stove –

RIVER. A lot of families are like that.

AVERY. *(Under their breath.)* A lot of families in the 1800s –

RIVER. Okay, did you not wanna come on our trip?

AVERY. Of course I did, we all did!

(The sound of a toilet flushing.)

But we just –

RIVER. You just what?

*(**PARKER** comes back on.)*

AVERY. WE DIDN'T REALIZE WE WOULD BE HIKING FOR TWO WEEKS.

(Beat.)

RIVER. I told you...

AVERY. A "long hiking trip" is a weekend for a normal person.

Most of the time people don't cross state lines!

PARKER. I've been wearing the same socks for a week.

RIVER. Well, then why do you guys stick around?!

AVERY. Because you need it!

> *(Beat.)*

RIVER. Need it?

AVERY. Not need it –

> Just we know you aren't going to –

>> (**RIVER** *plugs their ears and starts yelling.*)

RIVER. LA LA LA LA LA LA –

AVERY.	**PARKER.**	**RIVER.**
OH COME ON –	RIVER JUST –	LA LA LA

RIVER. *(Still yelling with their ears plugged.)* I AM GOING TO PEE. GOODBYE.

> (**RIVER** *goes into the bathroom.*)

> (**AVERY** *seems defeated.*)

> (**PARKER***'s confused.*)

PARKER. I thought we were going to talk to River together.

AVERY. I WANTED TO.

> I was going to.

> I just…

> I can't hold it in anymore, Parker.

> I love River, I do.

> Like seriously, but college isn't everything.

> And I wanted to, I really wanted to make this a fun trip and a fun goodbye –

PARKER. We're not using the G word.

AVERY. But that's what it is.

Parker, be realistic.

We're all going to different places, different schools.

And just because River isn't going doesn't mean I'm down to have hiked *(Checks their phone.)* 136 miles.

136 MILES.

PARKER. It's not that bad –

AVERY. My blisters have blisters.

And those blisters have blisters.

And those blisters have small red marks that are soon to be blisters.

My foot is a turducken of pain.

(**PARKER** *sits on the ground with* **AVERY**.)

PARKER. Do you want me to –

AVERY. Please massage my feet.

(**PARKER** *does.)*

PARKER. Look, I'm dying too.

I don't smell bad, I smell disgusting.

I literally feel like my body wakes up covered in stink and I have no way to fix that.

But come on, River's our people.

Ezra's our people.

Just cause we're going far away doesn't mean we're saying *(Mouthed.)* "goodbye."

It's a...see you later.

And I know that this trip wasn't...the plan.

BUT, we gotta be here for River, okay?

(**EZRA** *starts to walk back in with an armful of sports drinks.*)

AVERY. I know. I know.

I'm just dying.

(**EZRA** *doesn't realize* **AVERY** *and* **PARKER** *are on the ground.*)

(*They trip over* **AVERY** *and* **PARKER** *and drop bottles of sports drink everywhere.*)

EZRA. MY DRINKS.

PARKER. Oh my god, someone grab a –

(*Some of the drinks open and pool together into a puddle.* **AVERY** *lies down in it.*)

(*If the drinks don't spill,* **AVERY** *takes one, opens it, and pours it over their head.*)

(*They start laughing.*)

EZRA. Uh...what'd I miss.

PARKER. Avery told River we are dying.

I think they hit their breaking point.

EZRA. Oh no.

(*The sound of a toilet flushing.*)

(*No one notices.*)

PARKER. (*Softly.*) Avery.

Avery, you're scaring Ezra.

(*While* **AVERY** *breaks down,* **RIVER** *slowly comes out of the bathroom*)

AVERY. It's just...what else could go wrong!

What could be worse than being sticky and smelling like lemon melon kiwi for six more hours until I get to shower in a dirty river and sleep in a wooden shack with just a blanket you'd FIND COMPLIMENTARY ON AN AIRPLANE.

RIVER. Hi.

(Everything stops.)

*(**AVERY** looks up, covered in sports drink.)*

AVERY. River I didn't mean –

PARKER. Did you hear –

RIVER. I heard everything.

It's a bathroom in a grocery store, not a soundproof box.

(An uncomfortable beat.)

*(**EZRA** can't hold it in.)*

EZRA. I dropped all the –

RIVER. Yes, I can see you dropped all the drinks.

*(**RIVER** gets down and sits in the puddle of sports drink.)*

*(**MAEVE** comes in and sees the mess, but before she can say anything, she just listens to the conversation between the friends.)*

AVERY. What are you –

RIVER. I'm sorry.

I'm sorry to all of you.

I think I just wasn't happy with my college applications, and more than that, I don't wanna say goodbye.

*(**PARKER** gets on the ground and into the puddle.)*

PARKER. NO.

No, River, it's not a goodbye.

> (**EZRA** *also gets on the ground and into the puddle.*)

> (*A cuddle puddle.*)

EZRA. It's a see you later!

Of course I didn't want to go on a two-week hike.

I love air-conditioning.

RIVER. *(Laughing.)* I know you do.

EZRA. BUT I was happy to break my body because I know YOU love this!

In some...weird, painful way.

RIVER. You guys really didn't have to come.

PARKER. We wanted to.

RIVER. No, you didn't.

EZRA. We didn't.

AVERY. But we'd do anything for you.

I'd do anything for any of you!

> (**AVERY** *hugs all of them.*)

> (*A big group hug.*)

I'm sorry for what I said.

RIVER. You don't have to be.

I shouldn't have brought you all on this trip.

I shouldn't have made my mess your mess.

EZRA. Your mess is our mess.

We love you, dummy.

PARKER. You know what will make us all feel better?

AVERY. Six more miles of hiking and sleeping in a wooden hut!

EZRA. WOOHOO!

RIVER. No, no no.

AVERY. River, we're in the middle of nowhere!

We gotta finish now!

RIVER. I saw a motel down the road.

Let's go get a couple rooms.

Sleep all this off and then I'll get us bus tickets home tomorrow.

EZRA. MOTEL?!

LIKE BEDS?!

AND AIR-CONDITIONING?

AND TV?

PARKER. I COULD KISS YOU!

> (**PARKER** *kisses* **RIVER** *on the head.*)

> (*They laugh.*)

> (**MAEVE** *reveals herself.*)

MAEVE. So what's going on here?

EZRA. OH MY GOSH WE ARE SO SORRY!

RIVER. We spilled some drinks, we can totally pay for them!

AVERY. And help clean!

MAEVE. Don't worry about paying, but I have some cleaning supplies in the closet, and I could really use the help.

> (**EZRA, PARKER,** *and* **AVERY** *walk off to the closet.*)

*(**RIVER** pulls out their wallet.)*

RIVER. I really don't mind paying.

MAEVE. Seriously, don't worry about it.

I know how hard keeping friends after graduation can be.

Your people are good people.

Keep 'em close.

*(**RIVER** looks thankful.)*

(They start to go out toward their friends.)

MAEVE. Oh and I know the guy who owns the motel down the road.

He's nice, I'll give him a call and make sure you guys have a couple rooms on the house.

RIVER. Oh my gosh.

You don't have to do that –

MAEVE. Really, don't mention it.

Have a nice night with your friends.

*(**RIVER** goes off.)*

*(**MAEVE** feels satisfied.)*

(You can use the clean up of this scene as a transition featuring the characters from this scene or any employees that show up throughout the play.)

The Intercom: Lost in the Intercom

(The scene opens on a group of people in line at the one open register.)

*(**DALE** is checking out the last of **RITA**'s groceries on the conveyor belt.)*

*(**RONNIE**, a bagger, is configuring her items.)*

RONNIE. Paper or plastic?

RITA. Paper please.

RONNIE. You got it!

DALE. *(Still ringing.)* Got any big plans today?

RITA. It's my husband's birthday. *(Gesturing to the piling groceries.)* I'm making all of his favorites!

DALE. Well, happy birthday to him!

RONNIE. *(Holding up a wedge of cheese.)* Really nice stuff here, Rita.

RITA. Thank you!

I think I got everything…

(Looking things over and realizing) Oh shoot.

I forgot to get the jam!

DALE. Don't worry about it.

*(**DALE** grabs the corded phone from the side of the register and begins to speak over the intercom.)*

(While we see his mouth form the sentence "Can I get a runner over to pantry," what comes out of the intercom system is an incredibly loud and unintelligible garble.)

RITA. My goodness!

Dale, I think perhaps your intercom system is broken.

DALE. What do you mean?

RITA. Just that –

> (**KAYLA**, *a grocery store employee, cuts her off with her entrance.*)

KAYLA. What can I grab for you from pantry, Dale?

DALE. Rita, what type of jam were you after?

RITA. *(Confused.)* Oh, uh, raspberry, please.

KAYLA. Coming right up!

> (**KAYLA** *exits into the aisles for the jam.*)

> (**RITA** *remembers something else.*)

RITA. Oh, darn it, Dale, could you let her know we prefer the organic option Maeve has stocked?

DALE. You bet.

> (**DALE** *grabs the receiver again and we watch as he mouths, "Organic please, Kayla, thanks!" but what comes out is an even more violent and twisted sound than before.*)

> (**DALE** *and* **RONNIE**, *as well as the other* **CUSTOMERS** *in line, don't seem to clock this, but* **RITA** *nearly jumps out of her skin.*)

RITA. Dale!

> (*She gestures to the receiver.*)

What is that?!

DALE. Oh I know!

RITA. *(Relieved.)* You do?

DALE. Oh yeah, you almost never see these corded ones anymore, do you!

RONNIE. My grandma still has one like it.

RITA. No, that's not what I –

KAYLA. *(Entering with the jam.)* Here you are!

DALE. Thanks Kayla!

> *(**KAYLA** leaves.)*

RITA. How are you doing this?

RONNIE. Teamwork, I guess?

RITA. NO, I mean...

How can you understand anything coming out of that speaker?

It's awful!

DALE. It's not a concert hall, Rita, it's a grocery store.

Although I guess there's always room for improvement on my diction.

RITA. I – well – okay then.

DALE. *(Rolling his eyes.)* At least, that's what my choir leader is always telling mc.

RITA. Right.

Are we all ready to go?

DALE. *(Inspecting the jar of jam over in his hands.)* Gosh darn it...

RITA. What now?

> *(**DALE** and **RONNIE** share a look then at the same time say –)*

DALE & RONNIE. No barcode!

RONNIE. It happens sometimes with our farm-fresh inventory.

DALE. We are just really running poor Kayla all over town today aren't we?

RONNIE. I'll go this time!

RITA. Oh great, okay, thank you, Ronnie!

(Looking back nervously.) I'm so sorry to be holding up the line like this.

DALE. Oh no trouble, no trouble at all.

(To the line.) Hang tight, folks, I'll call in some backup!

> *(We watch as **DALE** picks up the receiver and says a quick "Can I get an additional ringer to the registers please?" but what comes out is the longest, most garbled, and perhaps borderline demonic sound yet. **DALE** smiles, completely unbothered by the fact that the noise is so loud or that it extends for a good long while after he's done speaking and has already hung up. **RITA** covers her ears and looks around in disbelief.)*

RITA. Now there's just absolutely no way someone can understa–

> *(**BILL** from "The Canned Goods Aisle" enters and waves at **RITA** and **DALE**.)*

BILL. Rita, Dale, sounds like you could use an extra set of hands up here.

> *(**BILL** heads over to another register, then grabs that one's receiver and mouths an "I can help you folks over on this register if you're ready." Of course, what comes out is a different, but equally unsettling and physics-breaking sound. The **CUSTOMERS** waiting behind **RITA** all have no issues understanding **BILL** clear as day and move over to his side. **RONNIE** returns.)*

RONNIE. Four ninety-nine, Dale.

DALE. *(Manually entering the price.)* Four, ninety, nine.

RITA. *(In utter disbelief, but ultimately, accepting.)* Four ninety-nine.

> (**RITA** *pays with her credit card.*)

RONNIE. And Dale, Maeve said that these are gonna be on special.

So go ahead and make another announcement.

RITA. HOW ARE ANY OF YOU –

> (**DALE** *begins another round of garble, the loudest and crunchiest yet.*)
>
> *(At its end, we hear over the intercom clear as day –)*

DALE. *(Through the intercom.)* – and thank you for shopping!

> (**DALE** *hangs up.*)
>
> (**RONNIE** *passes* **RITA** *the immaculately packed paper bags of groceries.*
>
> *(Beat.)*

RONNIE. Thank you for shopping!

RITA. Uh-huh!

> (**RITA** *exits.*)
>
> *(When useful, employ the device of the bad intercom to help provide coverage for transitions. It can motivate actors or crew members playing employees to action, as well as cause confusion for customers.)*

The Canned Goods Aisle:
You Don't Know (Pallet) Jack

(**BILL** *and* **CRAIG** *enter.*)

(**BILL** *points at a giant stack of boxes sitting atop a wooden pallet on the ground.*)

(**BILL** *points to the pallet, then off on the opposite side of the stage, indicating it needs to get moved.*)

(*Just then,* **BILL** *hears something on the intercom, gives a "one minute" motion to* **CRAIG***, then heads off.*)

(**CRAIG** *looks around. Looks at the towering pallet of goods.*)

(*He goes to one side of it and starts to push – the boxes topple immediately.* **CRAIG** *freaks out. This is his first day.*)

(*He begins restacking the boxes, but in his rush, keeps toppling them back down. He gets them stacked up tall again, then stands back, taking the situation in to strategize.*)

(*He gets an idea! Bending over, he reaches down to the bottom of the wooden pallet and starts to pull.*)

(*It's heavy, too heavy to budge.*)

(**CRAIG** *stands up in a huff. Wipes the sweat off his hands, and tries again, this time groaning through gritted teeth with the effort.*)

(*He loses his grip and tumbles back, landing flat on his back.*)

*(A **CUSTOMER** walks by; **CRAIG** quickly flips and pretends to be looking for a lost contact or earring.)*

*(The **CUSTOMER** offers to help but **CRAIG** waves them on. Phew. Now **CRAIG** is getting serious.)*

*(He looks both directions to check for **BILL**. Inspiration strikes again, but he'll have to be fast.)*

*(One by one, **CRAIG** starts stacking the boxes on the other side of the stage.)*

(When he's done, he races for the wooden pallet still on the ground on the original side, sets it up on the new side, then realizes he needs to restack everything on top again. He pulls his hair, slaps himself across the face, and gets back to work.)

*(Just as **CRAIG** finishes, sweating and out of breath, **BILL** reenters. He is wheeling on a pallet jack.)*

*(**BILL** looks around, confused.)*

(He could have sworn he left that pallet on this side of the aisle.)

*(He shrugs, crosses to **CRAIG**, and lifts the pallet with the jack, super easy.)*

*(**CRAIG** watches with pain in his eyes and a forced smile.)*

*(**CRAIG** gives him a thumbs-up and follows **BILL** off as he maneuvers the jack.)*

*(Whenever useful to you, employ **CRAIG** showing off with the pallet jack to help with transitions or provide coverage for changes.)*

The Produce Section: Mist Connections

(**NANCE,** *an eccentric woman with a flower in her hair, stands in the middle of the produce section.*)

(*She is on the lookout for someone, and gives a small, hopeful greeting to everyone who passes her by.*)

(*So far, it is mostly employees of the store, all wearing their matching smocks.*)

(*A* **PASSERBY.**)

NANCE. Oh hi –

(*Another* **PASSERBY.**)

Hello there!

(*Another* **PASSERBY.**)

Beautiful day...

(*Another* **PASSERBY.**)

Looking for any –

(**NANCE** *is left alone in the middle of the produce.*

(*She's dejected.*)

(*The sprayer system that mists the produce turns on. Then off.*)

(**NANCE** *lets out a big sigh.*)

(**ARTHUR,** *wearing a brightly colored T-shirt and holding a phone, enters and begins looking at apples.*)

Those are good.

ARTHUR. Excuse me?

NANCE. Sorry, I just – Those apples. They're good.

I picked some up last week.

ARTHUR. Oh, okay, thank you for the tip!

> *(There's a long silence as **ARTHUR** bags his apples and **NANCE** stands waiting.)*

Do you need help finding something?

NANCE. No, no…I'm just…

Waiting for someone actually.

ARTHUR. Okay!

> *(**ARTHUR** continues bagging apples.)*

> *(He reaches for greens under the misters next.)*

NANCE. He's late!

I think.

If he is coming, that is.

ARTHUR. Well that seems a bit impolite.

To leave someone waiting.

NANCE. He'll be here!

He should be on his way, I'm sure.

ARTHUR. Would you like to borrow my phone?

Make sure your person isn't having any car trouble?

NANCE. Oh, that's so kind!

But you see the problem is…

I don't actually have his number.

He's just supposed to find me by the flower in my hair.

NANCE. And I'll know him by his tan shirt.

(*As she is explaining, a group of* **EMPLOYEES** *pass by in their tan smocks. This line may be adjusted according to the costuming of your production's employees.*)

ARTHUR. Tan shirt, huh?

NANCE. So you see my problem.

ARTHUR. So this is like, one of those Missed Connections things?

NANCE. Exactly.

ARTHUR. I didn't think those still happened anymore!

NANCE. Well I just got so fed up with the whole online dating thing.

Trying all of the apps.

Feeling so disconnected from real life.

So I just said screw it!

I'm meeting someone in person or not at all!

And I started being intentional, wherever I went.

Trying to stay connected and engaged with the people actually around me.

ARTHUR. And how did it go?

NANCE. It was scary at first.

Then boring.

But then...something happened!

ARTHUR. What happened?

NANCE. I met someone.

Here, in produce!

ARTHUR. *(Joking.)* What'd you do, reach for the same apple at the same time?

NANCE. How did you know?

ARTHUR. Oh my gosh, I was just joking around –

NANCE. It was the apples!

It was those apples!

ARTHUR. Makes sense, whoever is placing this order wants a ton of 'em. They must be awesome.

NANCE. I reached for the shiniest one at the top of the pile –

ARTHUR. *(Getting into the cuteness of it all.)* And so did he –

NANCE. And when our hands touched, it was like –

ARTHUR. Electricity!

NANCE. Yes!

Exactly!

ARTHUR. That's so cute!

That's like, an actual meet-cute!

NANCE. I know!

So then we strike up a little conversation.

ARTHUR. And?

NANCE. And it turns out, we both have a favorite part of the grocery store.

ARTHUR. What's the part?

(The produce misters go off again.)

*(**ARTHUR** doesn't notice, too entranced by the love story.)*

*(But **NANCE** breathes in and out in time with them.)*

(She points.)

NANCE. The misters!

ARTHUR. The what now?

NANCE. The little spraying system they use to keep the produce from wilting.

ARTHUR. Oh yeah!

I used to love running over and sticking my hand into those as a kid!

NANCE. Some of us never stopped!

ARTHUR. So what happened next?

NANCE. He walked away.

ARTHUR. NO.

NANCE. I KNOW.

ARTHUR. But then how –

NANCE. I had to think of something.

I couldn't miss my chance at love!

ARTHUR. Right –

NANCE. Right so I'm walking around the store...

Feeling forlorn...

ARTHUR. Super forlorn!

NANCE. And this very intense gentleman in the floral section asked me why I looked so blue.

ARTHUR. Oh yeah, I know that guy, William!

I deliver a lot of flowers too, not just groceries.

NANCE. Well, I explained my situation to him and he suggested a Missed Connections ad.

*(**NANCE** pulls out a phone and shows **ARTHUR**.)*

ARTHUR. *(Reading.)* "Pink Lady seeking her Braeburn."

Oh that's really nice.

NANCE. I know, keep going.

ARTHUR. "We met on Monday in produce and I have not stopped thinking about our exchange. I loved connecting with you, and the passion that we share for the little things. If you're inclined, please meet me in the same place this coming Monday. I'll have a flower in my hair. We can make my famous apple crisp."

NANCE. *(Pointing to the flower.)* That was William's idea too. He's a real romantic!

ARTHUR. Did he respond?

(**NANCE** *scrolls down on the phone.*)

(Reading again.) "Pink Lady, I am so glad to hear from you! I loved our conversation and am glad to hear you felt the same. I will see you on Monday, wearing tan. I wouldn't mist it for the world!

"Yours, Braeburn"

Oh and he's funny too!

NANCE. I know! The total package!

ARTHUR. So...where is he?

(Beat. They look around.)

NANCE. Maybe it was too good to be true.

ARTHUR. No!

No! I refuse to believe that.

NANCE. Maybe it was silly.

Maybe I was just being silly.

ARTHUR. Stop stop –

ARTHUR. Wait, what's your name?

NANCE. Oh! It's Nance.

ARTHUR. Nance!

I'm Arthur.

NANCE. Nice to officially meet you, Arthur.

ARTHUR. But Nance, I refuse to believe this is your love story's end.

NANCE. There's nothing you can do.

But even just telling you about it was fun.

It was still a good day.

ARTHUR. Don't! Don't give up on me now, Nance.

I can find him.

NANCE. Aren't you busy?

(*She gestures to his shirt.*)

On a delivery or something?

ARTHUR. It can wait!

It's just some guy who's home sick.

You wait here for him while I do a lap of the store!

NANCE. (*Laughing.*) Okay Arthur.

(**ARTHUR** *runs off and disappears.*)

(*The misters turn on again.*)

(**NANCE** *rushes forward to catch the last few moments on her hands.*)

(*She smiles.*)

(*It is still a good day.*)

(A long, peaceful beat.)

(Then **ARTHUR** *comes in hot with several tan-smocked store* **EMPLOYEES***.)*

ARTHUR. Okay, take a good look at 'em!

NANCE. Arthur, what is this?

ARTHUR. A lineup!

NANCE. These aren't my Braeburn.

ARTHUR. *(Desperate.)* You're sure?!

NANCE. No.

But thank you for your help, everybody!

> *(The* **WORKERS** *all ad-lib "sure things" and "thank you for shoppings," collectively unbothered.)*

ARTHUR. So that's it?

He isn't coming?

NANCE. No. I don't think he is.

ARTHUR. You deserve better, Nance.

NANCE. And you deserve a raise!

Have a nice rest of your shift, Arthur.

I'm sure your customer needs his apples!

ARTHUR. Yeah, yeah.

Nice to meet you, Nance.

> *(***NANCE** *leaves.)*

> *(***ARTHUR** *sighs.)*

> *(He opens his phone and gets back on track, reading aloud to himself under his breath.)*

ARTHUR. Apples... Pink Ladies and Braeburns, got it.

Romaine and spinach...got it.

Special instructions...

"THERE WILL BE A BEAUTIFUL WOMAN WITH A FLOWER IN HER HAIR AT ONE OF THESE TWO LOCATIONS. TELL HER I'M ILL. BUT TO MEET ME NEXT WEEK!

"ALL MY LOVE...BRAEBURN"

(Beat.)

Oh.

My.

God!

(Joy spreads across his face as he breaks into a run after **NANCE**.*)*

(The stage is empty.)

(The misters start again.)